Millennial
Leap

Launching a Strategic, Citywide Youth Ministry Model for the 21st Century.

www.youthfront.com

ISBN: 0-967869-0-4

First Edition

Unless otherwise noted, Scripture taken from the New King James
Version. Copyright © 1983, 1975, 1971, 1966, 1965, 1964,
Harmony of the Gospels by Thomas Nelson, Inc.

Contents

Foreword

This book is a must read for every youth worker. It's a study guide. So grab your highlighter. Write in it. Learn from it. It's been written with passion and vision for young people in every community who need to know the Truth.

You may be relatively new to youth ministry or you may be like me... born into youth ministry, raised in youth ministry, and have worked in youth ministry your whole life. In either case, this book will give you exposure to the emerging new paradigm in youth ministry. It is a radical departure from the status quo of the traditional parachurch youth ministry... and a breath of fresh air for the youth workers who want to see all the students in their city hear about the love of Jesus.

Chapters 1-4 provide an important perspective for those who have not lived through the last 25 years of youth ministry. For us "old geezers" with 35 years or more experience, it is a great summary and reminder of what was very successful from the '40s through the '70s. Even though history can sometimes be a bit tedious for even the best of students, please don't give up on the book during these first few chapters. This background is critical to understanding the new model that is emerging today.

Beginning in Chapter 5, the intensity really picks up... building to a climax that gains momentum right to the very end – I say end, but it's not really the end. Most interestingly, this book isn't completely finished – you're invited to write the final chapter for yourself. Don't sweat it, you'll know what I mean when you get there.

Enough about the book – it's in your hands to explore for yourself... let me tell you about the author – Mike King.

Mike came to Christ through YouthFront's ministry just months before his high school graduation. Feverishly, he sought to win as many of his fellow athletes to Christ as possible before leaving high school. Because of the radical transformation that took place in his life, many listened and responded.

Having realized the life-changing impact of Christ on his young life, Mike joined our team immediately after high school with a quest to reach students with the Gospel. Even in those earliest days you could see that God had chosen Mike with all his raw talent and set him aside to be used greatly in missionary service to the youth culture around the world.

This was an early time in my ministry to young people as well. I remember challenging Mike to lock arms with our team and me for the long haul. Laughingly, we agreed to grow old, gray, and bald together reaching teenagers with the Gospel. So far we've succeeded at two out of the three. In the 25 years of that journey, this is what I've learned about Mike that defines who he is:

He never quits. He has seemingly endless energy. He's a hard worker, a fierce competitor, an innovative free-wheeling thinker – a risk taker. (While he has not yet parachuted from an airplane, he has bungied off what is purported to be the world's highest bungy jump in New Zealand with his 16-year-old son, Daniel.)

Mike is an excellent student. While working on our staff full-time, he completed his bachelor's degree and also holds a master's degree in counseling. He has an insatiable hunger for knowledge. He is a researcher and a strategic thinker with a Kingdom mindset. He believes his greatest textbook is the Bible – he has a passion for God's Word.

He's passionate. He's visionary. Mike's enthusiasm is contagious. He is motivational to the YouthFront staff and to the young people he minis-ters to. He's a team builder... and player. I know that Mike's personal mission statement is: To love God and to love others. I believe he's succeeding at this mission. His engaging personality and creative leadership style have made Mike a preeminent driving force throughout his tenure at YouthFront.

Mike is a devoted, faithful husband to his high school sweetheart, Vicki. Throughout his life, Mike's first ministry has always been to his family. He is a real example of right priorities. An unselfish father of three teenagers who love God and love our ministry, he has, through tears, watched them as they each have captured the vision of seeing their peers come to Christ. What could be a greater tribute to a man than to see his children following him in ministry?

Perhaps most of all, Mike is a romantic. Whether lost in Israel's occupied territories, (not good, trust me), or taking the cable car up to Sugarloaf in Rio de Janero, Brazil for the final night of a student missions trip, or crossing the border from Hong Kong to China with Bibles hidden under his clothes, it is, at times, more fun to watch Mike than to watch everything else going on. He is the first one to laugh at a joke, the first one to cry at a wonder-filled moment. Mike is one of the dreamers.

In the hierarchical structure of our ministry Mike technically reports to me – but I know in my heart that he is my partner – yoked together with Christ to make a difference in the lives of young people, not only in the greater Kansas City area, but also throughout the world. This book is hopefully, ultimately, with your help – for them.

Ronnie Metsker
President, YouthFront

Acknowledgements

This may be the toughest part of writing a book – properly acknowledging those who helped make it a reality.

I want to thank our entire staff at YouthFront. What a group of beautiful people – the joy of working together is difficult to adequately describe.

I want to thank the supporting churches of Kansas City involved in the effort to reach the youth of our city, the pastors, and especially the youth pastors in the YouthFront Alliance, working together for the Kingdom.

Specifically, I want to acknowledge the youth pastors in the Blue Springs, Missouri YouthFront Alliance network: Joey, Loyd, Gordon, Josh, Michael, Doug, Christopher, Ken, John, Bill, Eric, Stacey, and Erin. It's so great to be on the same team.

This project – entirely impossible without my closest friends and co-workers, the YouthFront Leadership Team. It saddens me that most people go through life without experiencing the camaraderie of a team of fellow laborers and friends who so thoroughly thrive on the joy of the journey together. Thanks Ronnie, Eric, Jim, Tim, Gorman, Topher and Jamie.

Thanks Ronnie for a quarter of a century friendship and partnership in ministry. You're a great leader.

Thanks to Topher and Jamie for challenging me to do this book and helping with the research.

Thank you Gorman, for the word-smithing, debates, and creative input.

Thanks Erin and Dawn for your creative and critical eyes.

Thanks Monte – your artwork is amazing.

Thank you Linda for all your help.

Mom and Dad, thanks for not giving up on your teenage son.

To my wife Vicki: thanks for being my best friend and lover for 25 years (all that, along with being my Administrative Assistant, WOW, you are incredible...) Thanks for all the time you spent typing and helping me finish this project.

To our three teenagers: Micah, Daniel, and Jessica – you make it easy for me to be a bragging father. Thanks for possessing a genuine faith; you give me credibility as a youth worker.

Thank you to Mark Senter for documenting the historic development of youth ministry in North America. The first two chapters of this book would have been impossible without your scholarly work.

I've never met you, but a thank you to Dallas Willard for writing *The Divine Conspiracy.* I have to agree with Richard J. Foster that it is, "The book I've been searching for all my life." Thanks for energizing a renewed passion to know Jesus intimately.

Since Christian youth societies were first
introduced in the 1700s, the development of
modern day youth ministry in the U.S. has
been increasingly progressive.

Introduction

Nothing has contributed as greatly to the pursuit of the Great
Commission over the past 300 years than youth ministry. The reason is
simple: youth ministry is effective. An overwhelming majority of those
who enter into a personal relationship with Jesus Christ do so before they
leave their teen years. Couple this well-established fact with this trend:
the youthfulness of the world's population is ever increasing. These fac-
tors alone should cause every church and youth group to prioritize and
expand their efforts to reach youth with the Good News of Jesus Christ.
That leaves us with a major question, what is the most strategic way to
meet this challenge?

Before we can answer that question, we need to look at where youth ministries have come from. After a brief look at its early development, this
book will focus on the evolutionary changes to youth ministries prevalent
during the 20th century. Finally, it explores the emerging movements and
models that will bring forth not evolutionary, but revolutionary changes
in youth ministry in the new millennium.

This is not a book of new methods on how to entertain youth. Nor is it
a book with a plethora of new creative program ideas. This book is for
those interested in the big picture of how youth ministry can become
more effective and efficient in the 21st century. Its focus is on new structures and paradigms for those engaged in youth ministry both in the
church and the parachurch.

The Youth Ministry Movement

A spiritual movement is...

The collective activity of committed, multiplying disciples as they band together and trust God for an impact greater than their own individual ministries. [1]

Bill Bright, Founder of Campus Crusade

Bill Bright's definition serves well to describe what is happening in many of our cities across the country. Youth workers are linking arms in strategic ministry partnerships to advance the evangelization of students. One such partnership blossomed into See You at the Pole. In 1989, a group of students became actively involved in a movement founded in prayer when a few teens circled around their school flagpoles to pray for their schools, friends and country. See You at the Pole was born in those solemn morning minutes. This student prayer movement continues to expand. On September 15, 1999 more than three million students started the school year praying around their flagpoles.

These teens quickly decided they wanted to pray together more than once a year. Since then, students have established thousands of on-campus clubs using rights established through the Equal Access Act. This students' emphasis of prayer coupled with the Equal Access Act is providing fuel for the emergence of a "New Movement."

Some readers will be threatened by the concepts in this book. My intention is not to irritate youth workers, but rather to encourage all of us to think dynamically. My hope and prayer is that this book and its message will capture your imagination, stir you to scheme and dream and, as God speaks to your heart, challenge you to create "new wineskins" to hold this new wine.

God is doing something unique and exciting that I believe will enable us to LEAP into a new millennium of possibilities. Are you ready?

SECTION 1

What Was

CHAPTER 1

The Beginning
Youth Ministry's Roots in North America

The Industrial Revolution had much to do with the development of specialized youth ministry. In an agrarian society, children were expected to become adults quickly because their assistance in running the farm was a necessity. If they were lucky, children went to school, but only until they were strong enough to be more useful on the farm.

The Industrial Revolution changed all that. People of all ages moved in droves from the farms into the cities where the jobs were. Instead of working on the farm children and teens began working in factories, often referred to as *sweatshops*, where working conditions were so bad for these young people that America's social conscience was soon stirred. As a result, child labor laws were passed to control the minimum employment age. In addition, compulsory school laws were passed requiring children to attend school. This suddenly created an extended and artificial transition from childhood to adulthood – now known as *adolescence* – that would last seven to ten years, or more. In short, a youth sub-culture was formed. However, it would take many years before this phenomenon was formalized.

A New Class

In the early 1900s, G. Stanley Hall was the first to describe the developmental period between childhood and adulthood as adolescence. Hall legitimized adolescents as a group of people with unique needs and challenges. It had taken nearly 200 years of social change in America to establish and finally name this unique developmental period of life, but it was one that would reverberate throughout the 20th century and unleash many repercussions worldwide. Today, few can imagine that there could ever exist a time when the term or concept of adolescence was unknown.

Early Days

Christian "youth societies" were introduced in the 1700s and flourished into the 1800s, laying the foundation for specialized youth ministries. These ministries would eventually boom in the 20th century and firmly establish youth ministry as a key tool for pursuing the Great Commission in the western world.

The first references of student organizations formed for the purpose of conducting ministry date back to the early 18th century. During a funeral sermon for a schoolteacher, the preacher Cotton Mather described how that teacher – along with some of his students – had formed a "Christian society at Harvard in 1706." [1] Years later, across the ocean in 1780 England, Robert Rikes created the concept called, *Sunday School.* His desire was to teach young people to read and learn the Bible. Within five years the idea had caught on in the United States when the adventuresome, American church-going public seized this concept of Bible training for youth. At first, American church leadership was threatened by the Sunday School idea, but by 1800 it was on its way to being synonymous with Sunday morning church attendance.

In 1844, twelve young men in London, England worked on a plan that would enable them to live out the Christian faith in their culture. They formed an organization called the Young Men's Christian Association, or YMCA. The purpose of their new organization was to share their faith and evangelize young men. It wasn't long before an American student studying in the U.K. brought the YMCA strategy home with him to Boston. By 1851, the YMCA had spread to the United States. Many YMCAs emerged from collegiate populations, which provided an excellent recruitment vehicle for young people to join the student volunteer movement. Over 20,000 students answered the call to foreign missions from this movement.

In the latter half of the 19th century, several church pioneers attempted to incorporate some of the components of the various Christian student movements into church associations. Unfortunately, most of these met with limited success. But there are some success stories, including that of a pastor from Portland, Maine – Francis Clark.

During the late 1870s, Francis Clark set the stage for successful youth ministry within local churches and denominations. Clark organized 70 young people from his church to stand against the wickedness of their culture. As a result of Clark's pioneering vision, Christian Endeavor was founded in February 1881 and, within 15 years, this youth program had been adopted by seven denominations, including the Presbyterian General Assembly, Missouri Synod Lutheran, and many Methodist, United Brethren, and Baptist churches. A new "youth ministry move-ment" had arrived.

The success of these new youth movements within their denominations - along with the YMCA and collegiate student ministries – led to an early 20th century explosion of youth social clubs with a Judeo-Christian foundation. The Boy's Club of America was founded in 1906, 4-H Clubs in 1907, Camp Fire Girls in 1910, Boy Scouts of America in 1910, and the Girl Scouts of America in 1912. All of these organiza-tions focused on utilizing adult volunteers whose primary goal was to mentor students and create outstanding citizens with high moral character.

School Daze

Before we jump into the 20th century with both feet, another event occurred – in 1875 – that would prove to be one of the most critical fac-tors in the development of our modern day youth ministry. The United States Supreme Court established the American public high school as a required part of the education system. Surprisingly, few could foresee the overwhelming effect this decision would have on youth: public school soon became the central focus in the lives of young people. Public school also became – and continues to be – a major dynamic in the development of youth ministry. Moreover, the role that public school plays in contemporary youth ministry will likely increase in the years ahead.

So hang on! We're about to jump into the 20th century.

> "They want me to make the kids sing hymns, but the kids want to sing choruses."
>
> *Dr. Al Metsker*

CHAPTER 2

The Parachurch Phenomenon

The Rise of the Youth Ministry Parachurch in the Mid-20th Century

The two hundred years of youth ministry endeavors during the 18th and 19th centuries were a countdown to the blast-off of aggressive youth ministry efforts in the 20th century. These 200 years laid the groundwork, but the undeniable growth of youth ministry in the last half of the 20th century was in many ways beyond human control. A sovereign God was at work through compelling circumstances that would catapult us through revolutionary events in the first half of the 20th century.

For example, the 1925 Scopes Monkey Trial attacked the fundamentals of the Christian faith. With it came immense publicity and widespread debate. Christian parents were understandably concerned about whether they could pass their values on to the next generation.

Where was the Local Church?

Moreover, congregations were too apathetic, or too busy, to focus resources on pioneering innovative youth ministry pursuits. The evangelical church was consumed with its own battle against liberal theology that had filtered out of Europe and was finding a home within mainline denominations. And no one can forget the Great Depression, which was a major challenge in itself and detracted any possible attempt to expand church outreaches.

The combined effects of liberal theology, the Great Depression, and two sobering World Wars were the wake-up call. The final bell toll was, as already noted, the institution of public school education, which quickly imposed a strong secular influence on impressionable young people. Over the next 15 years the ever-increasing secularization of public schools further intensified the need for a major youth ministry movement. The time was ripe for a spiritual awakening? Unfortunately, the local church didn't appear to be ready to facilitate this movement.

According to Dave Adams, Executive Director of the National Center for Youth Ministry, "little was happening in local church youth ministry (during this time) because the denominational machinery was not ready for the rapid changes that were taking place in youth work." [1] Not surprisingly, this void in church response would be the "mother of invention." God began raising up youth ministry pioneers who would step outside the boundaries of their churches and employ strategies to reach young people. The most obvious place, of course, would be to go where the need was greatest and where the largest concentration of youth assembled: Christian youth clubs began popping up in secondary schools all over America.

Stepping Up

Mark Senter, in his excellent, must-read book, *The Coming Revolution in Youth Ministry,* closely examines this period. Senter states,

> *Youth movements begin as unconnected responses to the needs of young people. When there is a period of social change, adolescents respond in ways that concern adults. Seldom do these godly people wait for someone halfway across the nation to provide a program. They simply begin doing something. Before long they discover that someone else has been ministering to young people in a similar manner and begin sharing insights and comparing notes, weaker strategies are dropped in favor of more effective methods, and in time a movement takes form.* [2]

They surely did "begin doing something." That something was the phenomenal establishment and growth of what would become known as the youth ministry *parachurch* (or outside-the-church) movement. This development would change forever how youth ministry was to be conducted.

The parachurch phenomenon exploded onto the scene. Innovative pioneers and entrepreneurs, many of whom had attempted to implement their ideas through the context of a local church but found themselves stifled by a denominational environment, were leading new organizations. These founders were fueled by a passion for the evangelism of youth, a job that was not getting done by or in the local church. Evelyn Mclusky established the Miracle Book Club in 1933; Jim Rayburn founded Young Life in 1940; and a handful of men led by Torrey Johnson organized Youth for Christ (YFC) in the early 1940s.

I had the privilege of being mentored by one of these pioneers. Dr. Al Metsker, the Founder and President of Kansas City Youth for Christ (KCYFC) took me under his wing when I was an 18-year-old, new believer. Dr. Al was one of the original founders of Youth for Christ, along with Torrey Johnson, Jack Wertzen, Percy Crawford, Bob Cook, and others.

I marveled at his stories of those early days. Dr. Al talked of how these men were surprised to find one other. When they compared notes, they discovered that each was involved in a similar ministry to youth that had sprung up spontaneously. During these meetings they decided to form Youth for Christ. Even when I arrived in the mid 1970s I could still feel the vibrations of his excitement as he described meetings that were held in the early 1940s. It was during one of these meetings, in 1945 at Winona Lake, that they hired a "young fireball" named Billy Graham to spread the Youth for Christ concept nationwide.

"Rallying" to the Cause

The most important and best-known event of Youth for Christ was the Saturday Night Rally. By 1950 the YFC movement was holding rallies in nearly 1500 cities. Mark Senter explains it:

> *Youth for Christ Rallies created a movement towards Christian service. Just as the American military had been the savior of the western world, American evangelicals viewed themselves as the saviors of the spiritual world.* [3]

After nearly twenty-five years of Saturday Night Rallies, the Youth for Christ movement began to focus on other strategies. By 1970, the famous Youth for Christ Saturday Night Rally had largely been abandoned in most cities. However, I will be forever thankful to Dr. Al Metsker for continuing these enthusiastic gatherings of students in Kansas City. In the spring of 1975, I heard my first clear presentation of the Gospel at a Kansas City Youth for Christ Rally. I was a senior in high school and far from God. I was amazed that 1500 students my age were excited about Jesus. I sat engrossed as Dr. Al stood on the edge of the stage, leaning to the point of almost falling off, as he enthusiastically preached the Good News. WOW! I was convinced.

And, like other cities across the United States, the Kansas City weekly rallies – filled with enthusiastic singing, skits, talented musicians, engrossing speakers and strong spiritual challenges – boasted weekly crowds of several thousand teenagers. Frequently during the year a *Super Rally* would be held with as many as 10,000 teenagers in attendance for a spiritual charge up. It was through these successful Youth for Christ rallies and evangelistic meetings that Billy Graham's crusades were birthed.

This phenomenon was a wave across the American landscape. The magnitude of its importance to 1960s' young people was demonstrated in the

1996 movie, "That Thing You Do," starring Tom Hanks. The story concerns the rise to fame of an early '60s Beatles-type rock group. As the group gains popularity, they discuss with a prospective manager the possibility of performing at "roller-rink dances, Youth for Christ Jamborees and rock and roll shows." [4] Soon Youth for Christ and another organization, popularly known as FCA, had become household names, highly prominent even outside Christian circles.

FCA, or The Fellowship of Christian Athletes, was birthed in Pittsburgh during the mid-1950s. Its growth was explosive. Sports and music were, and continue to be, of major interest to young people. While other youth ministry parachurch organizations utilized music as a primary tool, FCA perfected the use of athletics to reach students. High school coaches became Huddle leaders to mentor student athletes. By 1960, over five million students were involved in YFC clubs, FCA Huddles, Young Life, and other similar groups that were meeting weekly across the country. In addition, these clubs trained tens of thousands of adult lay leaders to work with students. It is breathtaking to consider the staggering sum of people (both youth and leaders) whom God led to this movement.

Although these youth groups were formed outside the local church, they still relied heavily on churches, not only recruiting adults to work with students but counting on the church's financial resources to fund their aggressive efforts. Not surprisingly, as the parachurch movement slowly broadened its scope beyond youth to homeless shelters, mission ministries, and maternity homes (to name a few), tension between local churches and parachurch organizations mounted.

The Name Sticks

The last few pages have briefly reviewed the 20th century parachurch movement, which began in the post-World War II years. However, the label parachurch that describes ministries outside the direct church control did not come into vogue until the late 1960s. Since then, the parachurch movement has garnered a school of evangelists, philosophers, and statisticians, all eager to study and grow this phenomenon. Many of these experts cite the extraordinary success of parachurch ministries. For example, in the informative book, *The Prospering Parachurch*, the authors believe that "the Parachurch has been the representative organization for evangelicalism during the last 50 years." [5] And David Barrett, a church growth expert, reveals some surprising statistics: financial giving to parachurch ministries has now surpassed gifts to traditional churches, $100 billion to $94 billion respectively. Furthermore, the gap in money raised into the next millennium by these two groups will continue to widen. [6]

However, while some segments of the parachurch will continue to grow and prosper, it is my personal belief that the *youth ministry* parachurch movement has begun a rapid and inevitable decline. The good news, however, is that out of this and other significant trends a new and unique youth ministry model is emerging just in time for a new millennium.

SECTION 2

What Is

CHAPTER 3

The Local Church Responds
A New Position – Youth Pastor

Americans have, over the past few decades, become very aware of – and sensitive to – the needs of youth. We pass laws to protect and defend them, we organize programs to enrich them. We encourage listening to what they have to say and counsel parents and caregivers on relationships with them. None of this seems like a big deal today. But it was a big deal in 1943 when Dr. Al Metsker, founder of Kansas City Youth for Christ, wanted to organize youth rallies that included different churches. The idea was unheard of – and many within the local church thought the idea was a bit too radical.

Most of the early pioneers of the parachurch youth ministry movement were heavily involved in their local churches. These visionaries tended to be different in their style and approach to youth. As a result they met opposition. The church leadership even disliked Dr. Al's multi-colored bright socks and crazy ties! Why? Dr. Al, along with other aggressive and innovative entrepreneurs, seemed to threaten the status quo of the existing institutions. For Dr. Al, who was driven by his passion to reach lost teenagers, the decision became painfully obvious: he would have to form an independent organization where he would have the freedom to provide innovative youth ministry. And he was not alone; many youth leaders were forced to pursue their God-inspired vision outside the local church.

With their overwhelming success, it didn't take long before several organizations such as YFC and FCA gained respect through popular approval. Of course, as youth ministry parachurch organizations rapidly grew, they quickly caught the attention of the local church, where many of the more outreach-oriented churches recognized the contribution these ministries were making in the lives of their students. But only the most visionary churches in larger urban centers stepped up to employ full-time youth directors. Vista Community Church in San Diego, California and the Moody Memorial in Chicago, Illinois were among the first handful in 1948 and 1949, respectively. [1]

It would be another decade before full-time youth pastor positions would appear in larger metropolitan churches. Some smaller, leading-edge churches, which also saw a need to maintain the interest of their young people, began to experiment by hiring college or seminary students to work as temporary, part-time youth directors. Unfortunately, this strategy created a problem that has only recently subsided. Mark Senter explains:

> *Most church people – laymen as well as pastors and professors – saw the position of youth worker as a transitional one. Youth ministers were viewed as novice ministers who were gaining enough experience to qualify them for "real ministry." That is, the preaching pastorate. Youth ministry was considered an extension of one's education, a type of internship.* [2]

By the mid-1950s, nearly 200 U.S.-based denominations acknowledged the importance of youth ministry. A majority of these denominations employed denominational youth workers who spread the good news of youth work to their individual churches. At first, most relied on recruiting lay adult youth coordinators. With little or no formal training, these volunteers nonetheless dove into youth ministry, making an impressive effort to get involved in the lives of students.

When I arrived on staff at Kansas City Youth for Christ (KCYFC) in 1975, there were very few youth pastors in Kansas City. I personally can't recall more than five or six. Today, there are several hundred youth pastors in the Kansas City area. What an immense change! It's almost viewed as a necessity today (not only in Kansas City but across the entire country) for a church of 200 or more to employ a professionally trained, full-time youth pastor.

While this development is something to rejoice over, the dynamic change in youth ministry eventually led to considerable conflict between the para-church and the local church. At first and quite often, these relationships were a win/win situation for both the parachurch and the local, denomi-national church. Everyone was gaining and growing, especially the youth. The thriving youth ministry parachurch organization of the 1960s and early 1970s offered training to these church volunteers. The parachurch was also eager to *recruit* them in their mission to reach youth. Unfor-tunately, from the mid-70s, friction increasingly developed.

The conversation was something like this...

PARACHURCH: *Hey local church, you need us! We know how to do evangelism. We're focused, you should join us, we're in the big leagues.*

LOCAL CHURCH: *We are the church, we are God's chosen, you are stealing our kids. Go away!*

This was a tough situation, no doubt. However, conflicts, crises, and chal-lenges can be helpful if they force us to examine, evaluate and develop more effective and efficient ways to function.

By the 1980s, the youth ministries within the local church had grown while the emphasis on youth ministry in the parachurch began to show the first signs of gradual decline. It became increasingly obvious that somehow the parachurch and church needed to figure out how to get along. Finally, the two sides began to acknowledge a need to make a gen-uine, spiritual attempt to play on the same team. The spark to explore ways to work together to reach youth was lit.

> " May they be brought to complete unity to let the world know that you sent me. "

John 17:23, NIV

Chapter 4

The Birth of Networking
Youth Workers Begin to Connect

The turbulent 60s further convinced concerned Christian adults of the importance in reaching their young people with the Gospel. In response, youth ministry parachurch organizations climbed to their zenith during the 1970s. At the same time and by the same catalysts, local churches awakened to their need for youth pastors, a trend that would escalate through the decade. An illusory race had begun.

Tension between the parachurch and local church grew in intensity. Perceived competition and lack of communication fueled the animosity. Certainly, the inexperience and youthfulness of youth workers in both the church and the parachurch played a significant role in the situation. However, it is more likely that the greater problem was the inward fixation youth workers had on each other. Instead of focusing on the monumental task to reach a lost generation of students, too many youth workers obsessed on their perceived competition: other youth workers.

Many of the more mature youth leaders – within both the parachurch and local church – began to speak as prophets with a call for unity. It was difficult to ignore God's plea for unity among His believers because He made it so clear throughout the New Testament. The night before He was to be crucified, Jesus prayed in the Garden of Gethsemane. He petitioned the Father:

That all of them may be one, Father, just as you are in me and I am in you. May they also be in us so that the world may believe that you have sent me. I have given them the glory that you gave me, that they may be one as we are one: I in them and you in me. May they be brought to complete unity to let the world know that you sent me and have loved them even as you have loved me.

John 17:21-23, NIV

The call for unity by youth leaders had some effect, but the idea of *complete unity* that Jesus prayed for would prove to be a real challenge.

The Call

Networking provided a platform for both parachurch youth workers and church youth pastors from various denominations to check each other out. Early attempts were very cautious and fragile. Many of these networks were organized or facilitated by parachurch ministries, too often with a "we can help you on *our* terms" mentality. To say the least, the trust level was weak. Even if youth pastors wanted to take cooperation to a deeper level, most church leadership wanted this cross-denominational, parachurch networking to only go so far.

I still hold many memories of those infant network meetings and the ever-present baggage of immaturity and below-the-surface mistrust. The dream of strategic, innovative Kingdom building through cooperative network partnership would take years of foundational work.

However, in 1979, two dozen youth ministry leaders gathered to explore how youth workers could function together more effectively to reach students. This group continued to meet, and by 1981 they organized the National Network of Youth Ministries. Led by Paul Fleischmann, this organization preached the message of youth workers networking together.

Early networking expectations were minimal, usually focusing on the cultivation of friendship with other youth workers. Of course, the networking relationship was enhanced when youth workers began praying together. However, during these first few years, networking's best results occurred when youth workers actually cooperated on an event together – even though this wasn't the primary focus during the formative years.

The criteria for successful early networking had to remain simple. Networking would first have to go through an infancy stage before it could move into adolescence and eventual adulthood. John Crosby, an author and pastor, recommended several steps for developing an active youth worker's network. [1]

1. The idea of working together must be a felt need by more than one person.

2. Identify potential members.

3. Discern the fuzzy line between your agenda and the needs of the group.

4. Locate your common ground, and clarify your expectations.

5. Encourage members to participate selectively.

6. Set a fixed time for your meeting.

7. Make this an opportunity to pray for one another.

While this list was good for an infant network in Crosby's decade (1980s), it falls short of the potential that unified youth workers could experience in true Kingdom building.

One of the most common purposes fulfilled during this stage of youth ministry networks was that it provided a vehicle for youth workers to commiserate about the challenges they struggled with. Network meetings also seemed to be the place where you could boast to your peers about the exciting victories you experienced and the thrilling upcoming events you had planned. Though I'm sure I sound critical regarding this infant stage of networking, it was, no doubt, a necessary process to go through. Perhaps I was impatient. But I had also become increasingly aware that our work was much bigger and more urgent than these tiny steps would serve. As we moved into the 1990s it was time to grow up.

> **"**When I was a child, I talked like a child, I thought like a child, I reasoned like a child. When I became a man, I put childish ways behind me.**"**
>
> *I Corinthians 13:11*

CHAPTER 5

Networking Grows Up
The Maturing of Modern-Day Networks

The typical life span for organizations is approximately 40 years. So naturally we were thrilled to celebrate the 50th anniversary of our parachurch youth ministry, Kansas City Youth for Christ (KCYFC), in 1993. While that was a great year of ministry for us, a sensed wariness cloaked us as we observed the vast landscape of innovative youth ministry concepts. We became increasingly aware that our parachurch youth ministry model was in decline.

KCYFC's 100 full time staff members were not content with maintaining the status quo. We knew that the days when we were the only youth workers in town were over. We also knew that we had to create an environment where we could work arm-in-arm with the church. We talked openly and aggressively about a paradigm shift that would allow us to discover and participate in the next wave of innovation within youth ministry.

There were a couple of youth worker networks in Kansas City, primarily through involvement with the National Network of Youth Ministries. Through interactions with these groups, we could sense that youth worker networks were beginning to move beyond infancy and could become an integral part of future youth ministry strategies. Furthermore, our surveys discovered that 75% of youth workers desired interdenominational interaction, a fact that was consistent with an independent survey (February 1996) that revealed more than 80% of youth workers wanted to network. [1] The decision was clear: we made the development of these networks a priority.

Unfortunately, the church and the parachurch ministries were significantly at odds in the early 1990s. In an attempt to overcome this tension, we literally *gave* the National Network of Youth Ministries one of our most experienced, veteran youth workers, Roy Bilyeu. We continued to pay his salary but put him "on loan" with no strings attached. His sole purpose was to serve youth workers and form networks. And he did.

When Josh MacDowell organized See You at the Party in March 1993, youth workers across the country came together in unprecedented numbers to participate in this event. In Kansas City alone, over 200 youth workers joined together to simultaneously train nearly 4,000 students for evangelism. The result? Over 12,000 students came to The K.C. Party, and nearly 900 accepted Christ as Savior. Youth workers were energized. But soon the euphoria ended; the network lost the enthusiasm and momentum it had gained through the process.

It was unfortunate that the success of youth ministry networks seemed to rise and fall around events that could capture the attention of participants. Up then down, up then down – youth worker networks were clearly going through an adolescent stage. The networking idea had taken hold; we just had to find ways to sustain it. Youth workers across the country were more and more willing to come together and cooperate. It was only a matter of time before a new concept developed that would grab the imagination of youth workers and lead them to the commitment necessary to usher in mature, grown-up networks.

Although the Federal Equal Access Act had been passed in 1984, it took another decade for youth workers to figure out how to apply the opportunity created by the law. When Equal Access clubs began sprouting up in schools, especially those that were local church-focused and not para-church-focused, youth pastors were given a strategic purpose to network on a regular basis.

In 1996 there were four youth pastor networks in Kansas City that involved approximately 40 youth workers. In an attempt to serve the local church, KCYFC launched Club121, a church-centered, campus-focused, Equal Access program. Our role was to facilitate the youth pastor's success through his or her ministry to students on campus. Within months, 20 youth pastor networks were founded that actively involved 200 youth workers.

In late 1998, in a four-day symposium at Niagara Falls, I met with city-wide youth ministry leaders from around the country. As we discussed what God was doing in our individual cities, we quickly sensed that we were on "holy ground." Awestruck, we realized God was doing amazingly similar things simultaneously in our cities. The key vehicle for the moving of God in these cities was a common dynamic: a newly matured youth ministry network that generated a purpose-driven, cooperative, and strategic ministry.

We discussed our individual experiences within the development of the youth worker networks and described the trends in these emerging partnerships. We noted the differences between what youth ministry networks have been and where we believe God is taking them. They include the following:

Old Networks	Emerging Partnerships
My Kingdom	God's Kingdom
Pastoral Leadership	Apostolic Leadership
Network (in order) to Get	Partner (in order) to Give
Parachurch/Denominational	Citywide Organized
Personal Agenda	Kingdom Agenda
Come (for an event)	Go (to do ministry)
Information	Innovation
Centralized	Decentralized
Programming Events	Pursuing God's Plan
Accomodation	Reconciliation
Seeking His Hand	Seeking His Face
Parachurch Leadership	Interchurch Leadership

There can be no doubt: God is at work across the nation, and a move-ment is emerging that will change forever the way youth ministry is to be done.

SECTION 3

The Threshold

> "Speed is useful only if you are running in the right direction."[1]
>
> *Joel Arthur Barker*

CHAPTER 6

Dynamic Forces
Unstoppable Contemporary Waves of Change

A maelstrom of dynamic trends, undercurrents, forces and events all contribute in both small and large ways to how youth ministry will be conducted in the future. Clearly, we are in the midst of numerous revolutions that interrelate to create synergy in one of the most powerful times in human history: technology, business, cultural, social and spiritual forces are driving intense change. And there's no doubt, they have and will continue to have an impact on the way youth ministries interact and network to bring the Good News of Jesus Christ to teens throughout the world. This chapter highlights just a *handful* of these forces.

New Technology

> *Now the whole earth had one language and one speech.*
>
> *Genesis 11:1*

No one is immune – technology is definitely changing the way we live our lives. It is increasingly more difficult to keep up with technological advancements. The Internet is an excellent example. Tom Peters in his book, *Circle of Innovation*, proclaims, "We are in the midst of the most profound change since the beginning of the Industrial Revolution, over two centuries ago."[2] Peters emphasizes that the Internet, which has caused the death of distance, will be one of the most significant forces of change shaping society over the next 50 years.

I recently conducted a YouthFront International Training Conference for youth workers in Hong Kong. As part of my normal, daily routine I logged onto the Internet from my hotel room to retrieve and send e-mail. Within a few seconds I was in a "flash session" with seven youth workers and staff in Kansas City. Suddenly, an eighth person, a fellow staff person who was in the hotel room next door to me, joined our conversation. While we "talked" I was struck by the realization that I was communicating just as easily with youth workers 8,000 miles away as with a colleague twelve feet away. Distance is dead!

During that conference I also received the same e-mail communications that all 375 youth workers in Kansas City were sent. I read victory reports, updates on our upcoming dcTalk concert, news of three new Club121s, information about a youth pastor's appreciation banquet, and other bits from the daily (sometimes hourly) happenings back home. It was almost as though I had been sitting in my office in Kansas City!

Technology creates great opportunities to communicate with students. Today's teenagers, or *Millennials*, are comfortably "plugged in." "They communicate effortlessly by e-mail, use cell phones, VCRs and CD-ROMs without thinking about it." [3] And in Kansas City, Christian students and youth pastors are linked through a website, where they share their campus ministry stories, victories and prayer requests.

After KCYFC established its website, www.youthfront.com, we were astounded by the first monthly "traffic" report. Over 135,000 hits (visits) were made in one month! The really amazing thing is that because the website was under construction, we hadn't really promoted it. The following e-mails were pulled off the YouthFront website. They represent the communications possibilities that did not exist even five years ago.

I am one of the Student Leaders in my Club121.
Being in this position is an AMAZING thing for me!
I love showing up every week at our meetings and
seeing all these kids from my school who want to
know Christ… Sadly, school is coming to an end, and
Club121 will be over… Our Club's goal is to reach
121 people. So far we haven't reached that goal
yet, but I'm asking you, all of you who read this,
to pray for our Club… I'm just writing to tell you
all how much of a wonderful event this has been for
me. If your school doesn't have a Club121, I
strongly urge to try to form one in your school next
year. Talk to your pastor or youth minister. Try
your hardest, I PROMISE you, it will be worth it.
Good luck to you ALL!

Live-4-God
Crystal
8th grade

Lincoln Prep High School Club121 had a pizza and rap
music session in the school cafeteria. There were
71 teens in attendance. Teens from a neighboring
high school - Northeast/KCMO - came and rapped, then
the Club121 video was presented, followed by a presentation of the Gospel… 13 teens responded by coming
forward and praying the sinner's prayer.

Jack
YouthFront Area Coordinator

This morning was "Super Natural" at the West Platte
Club121. We watched a video that talked about the
lifeboats from the Titanic. One boat had twelve
people in it, even though it could hold up to forty.
But, they didn't go back to save any of the people
that were in the water. They were safe and they
didn't want to risk their own life to save someone
else. This was a picture of how we are sometimes in
our faith in Christ. If we are saved, we don't want
to take a chance and share with anyone else. Well,
this morning I challenged the kids to get out of

their life-boat (the classroom) and go out into the
water (the hallways) and save some of their friends.
Thirty kids left the boat; forty-seven ended up in
the room when they came back. There were even kids
standing in the hallway looking in the door. It was
too cool! Eight kids were pulled from the icy
waters of sin and separation. God is large and in
charge! Later in the week, I coincidentally met the
father of one of the girls who accepted Christ.
This may be the first step to getting this family
connected to our church.

Brady
Youth Pastor
Club121 Coach

This kind of communication among students and youth pastors from all over Kansas City creates a feel of connection to a citywide movement.

According to George Barna's research, "It is estimated that by the year 2010, 10-20 percent of Americans will derive their spiritual input – and output – through the Internet" [4] Gerald Celente also speculates on the future potential of this new technology, "By 2010, for the first time since the fall of the legendary Tower of Babel (Genesis 11) – a single universal language will exist on earth." [5] This universal communication will be via the Internet and will be a strategic component in carrying out the Great Commission.

Greco-Roman developments set the stage for the early church to advance its cause. The Greeks provided the world with a common language and the Romans linked the world through their construction of a transportation network.

Reggie McNeal states it succinctly:

The book of Acts records the spread of the faith – along Roman roads connecting old Greek cities – to Gentile populations. That we are today members of a global community is not news. This is a fact. People are literally only a few keystrokes removed from any point on the planet. Today, as in the first century, cultural diversity makes fertile ground for Gospel sowing and reaping. The challenge for North American Christianity involves a willingness to emerge from a sociological cocoon and adopt a missional agenda designed to embrace the world. [6]

"A new generation of computer literate people will communicate instantly with one another on equal footing." [7]

Gerald Celente

This technology is largely available to all, so we don't necessarily need to be "techies." But we do need to be prepared to apply the technology strategically. Most importantly, "How the organization deploys its technological assets and resources to achieve differentiation will make the difference in whether it is successful." [8]

We simply must not be afraid of technology. Technology can be one of our greatest tools as we move forward in our efforts to fulfill the Great Commission.

New Leadership Trends

Strategic planning, empowerment, team building, thinking outside the box... these are the buzzwords for a new style of management. Organizations are reinventing how they lead and manage. Over the last ten years, ministry leaders have also been challenged to learn from the professional world and become more strategic in their leadership. This dynamic is a major factor to guide ministry leaders to focus on the bigger picture – getting the job done.

Willow Creek Community Church in Chicago led the way by challenging church leaders to grasp the importance of strategic, purpose-driven ministry. Bill Hybels did a masterful job in showing how professional, spirit-led leadership could greatly enhance ministry efforts. I remember fondly the hours we spent, during the early 1990s, with Bo Boshears and Troy Murphy, youth leaders at Willow Creek, as we began to question our role as a parachurch youth ministry. They asked us a lot of difficult *why* questions. I remember the embarrassment of not always knowing why we were doing what we were doing. Bo and Troy, along with many other people, incidents, conferences, books, tapes and seminars changed the way we viewed our to approach ministry.

Our Leadership Team spent hundreds of hours wrestling with "Mission," "Vision," "Values," "Strategic Plans," etc. We began an intensive training program for our staff. We began to focus on what we were *accomplishing* instead of what we were *doing* A wholeness settled over our organization and prepared us for the kind of effective and efficient ministry we had never before experienced.

Mission, vision, values, and being *purpose driven* have become fundamental building blocks in today's youth ministry and will continue to be enormous factors in the development of cooperative youth ministry efforts in the future.

The New Millennium

As the 20th century drew to a close, we heard a great deal of noise about the new millennium – some scares, some promises, but mostly speculation as to its pending effect on current and future generations. Personally, I feel it has fueled an openness among youth ministries to network more strategically.

While prophetic speculation centering specifically on the year 2000 has been dismissed by a majority of believers as erroneous biblical interpretation, it has subtly, almost subconsciously caused many to evaluate the effectiveness of their ministry efforts. The many troubling issues we face as we begin this new millennium – terrorism, ethnic conflicts, biological/chemical warfare, genetic engineering – all add to the climate of uncertainty. These issues lead to comments such as, "we need to join together while we still have time" or "we need to work together before it's too late," and have certainly contributed to an openness to partner for ministry. And even though these catalysts appear to be both a desperate urgency and an acknowledgment of startling upheavals in the world, they are facilitating a powerful and hopeful message!

New Student Revolution

Another factor pushing youth workers to join together is the example set by the students themselves. Students are not inclined to getting hung up on denominational issues, sectarian labels, or differences. They just naturally come together on campus as the Body of Christ. Our students can work together; shame on us if we can't.

We only need to look at See You at the Pole to see over three million students excited about joining together to serve God. With the rapid growth of new Equal Access clubs on campus – through such efforts as Challenge 2000, Youth Alive, FCA and First Priority – youth workers are sensing the need to join forces and facilitate this student-led movement.

Challenge 2000 is an effort of the National Network of Youth Ministries comprised of nearly 60 denominations and youth ministry organizations working together in cooperation. The Challenge 2000 campaign has been adopted as the youth arm of the Mission America campaign. Challenge 2000 has set a goal of sharing Christ with every student in grades 7 through 12 by establishing a student-led ministry in every school by December 2000. Efforts like these truly stoke the fire of strategic networking partnerships.

Post Modernism

There's no reason to spend a great deal of time documenting the social environment that exists because of the development of post-Christian, post-modern cultural trends. What matters most is that post-modern youth want to be involved in something meaningful, something that will make a real difference in the world. Our unwillingness as youth workers to come together and work in unity will pour cold water on Christian students' willingness to mobilize as the body of Christ on their campuses and leave them cynical of our pettiness.

Dave Urbanski, editor of *YouthWorker Journal*, says,

> On the most basic level, post-moderns (including those folks populating your youth rooms) have rejected the black-and-white, cognitive, and scientific ideas that have characterized much of the modern era... They have replaced them with qualities such as relative truth, cynicism, and information overload... The most important thing to keep in mind is that the post-modern heart is ready like no generation before it to hear-and embrace-the Gospel. [9]

Gerald Celente, director of the Trends Research Institute in Rhinebeck, New York, calls these students a "revolution in waiting." [10] He goes on to say that the Millennials (or post-modern generation) are the first generation since the Boomers to be activists. He's right! Our Christian students living in this postmodern society *can* lead a revolution. They are willing to take a stand. They will respond to our coaching if we present them with a big-picture plan of Kingdom building.

It's important to acknowledge that students today receive the message of the Gospel far more easily when it is *demonstrated* in the changed life of a peer rather than in a cognitive encounter with the claims of Christianity. In *Generation Next*, George Barna proclaims *pragmatism* as the key for Christian students to capture a grand vision. If our strategies to reach students are not effective, they will reject them as irrelevant. If the strategies and programs are effective in reaching their friends, they will embrace and commit to them. It bears repeating: they want to be part of something that works. In addition, new methods must be employed to reach students who struggle with the concept of absolute truth and readily accept relativism.

New Challenges

As our culture's Judeo-Christian foundations crumble, it becomes increasingly clear how foolish it is for the church to be divided. Fortunately, the church of Jesus Christ is waking up to the importance of unity. Christians are realizing who the enemy is... and it's not the church down the street.

We need to work together to counter the enemy's attack. I believe the huge shift in the church in North America over the last 15 years is founded in a new zeal to obey Jesus' challenge to engage the culture and be the "salt and light."

Youth workers see the truth – they are joining hands and rallying around the banner of passion for non-believing students by identifying their culture and using it to reach others with the Good News of Jesus!

> **"The** current generation of teenagers doesn't have denominational affiliation. Students move across party lines without second thought. Teenagers connect to causes, not denominations...**"** [1]
>
> *Monty Hipp, denominational youth leader for the Assemblies of God*

CHAPTER 7

Declining Denominational Influence and the Perishing Parachurch

The Way We Were...

The age of the oldest parachurch youth ministry organizations falls into the 50-60 year range. As mentioned earlier, the average life span of an organization of any kind is approximately 40 years. Most organizations simply lose focus and energy over time. The youth ministry parachurch movement is no different: it too is in decline. *But, take heart! This dynamic is at work creating perfect conditions for the birth of a new youth ministry movement.*

Why do most organizations fail over time? Sometimes the organization is structured so much around the founder's personality or charisma that it fails to thrive as the organization transitions to the second generation. In some cases, the parachurch youth ministries have strayed from their original mission. Others have failed to adapt to changing times. Mike Yaconelli of Youth Specialties is direct in his appraisal:

> *I believe we're in a crisis of youth ministry. Most of our models of parachurch youth ministries were developed in the 1940s, 1950s and 1960s and are out of touch. When I talk to their staffs they get angry and defensive. I'm sorry. I wish I could say it's a golden age and everything is going great but it's not. We must focus on how kids really are today not dwell on what we were or did in the past.* [2]

Surprisingly, the leading factor in the decline of youth ministry parachurch organizations is actually good news. They have fulfilled their true purpose – awakening the local church to the importance of embracing youth ministry. Remember, by the middle of the 1980s, the local church had responded and since then has been doing a much better job of evangelizing, equipping and empowering students. Mark Senter writes:

> To make matters worse for YFC (but better for the kingdom of God), churches have flattered the movement by imitating its strategies and methods. At the same time, they have recruited youth ministers from the same resource pool as YFC previously did, the Christian colleges and Bible institutes. Since church paid salaries and YFC required staffers to raise support, churches were able to attract and hold an increasingly large number of more creative youth workers. In many ways, Youth for Christ has done its job so well that its niche in the ecology of youth ministry has been taken over by the very people it spawned. [3]

Recently, Wesley Willmer and David Schmidt wrote a book called *The Prospering Parachurch*. In it, they contend that the parachurch is alive and well. For example, the parachurch has just surpassed the local church in money raised for Kingdom work – $100 billion to $94 billion. It might appear at first that my view of the youth ministry parachurch in decline is a contradiction of their findings. Not so. The authors stress that the current parachurch is succeeding by doing what the local church is *not* necessarily doing (homeless shelters, feeding the hungry, etc). This used to be true about youth ministry, but again, the local church has responded here.

One of the purposes for writing this book is to challenge existing parachurch youth ministry organizations to do a paradigm shift and redesign how they do ministry. I believe the parachurch organizations that are willing to take the risk to evaluate what they are doing and change in light of the future will play a significant role in the emerging youth ministry structure of the 21st century.

Ivory Towers Falling

The decline in denominational influence is another dynamic that is helping to create an environment for an emerging movement. I became aware of this problem early on, before it appeared in magazines, journals, or books. The first sign occurred when churches began dropping the denominational label in their church name. Of course, local churches changing their names is not necessarily a sign of conflict within the denomination – it's far more hopeful than that! Many denominations encourage their churches to change their name because the leadership is more concerned about building the Kingdom than the denomination.

Hanging around youth pastors and hearing them voice their feelings about denominational loyalty and expectations has reinforced my observations. There seems to be a general consensus among youth pastors that youth ministry materials, concepts and ideas within the denominations are coming from those who aren't necessarily doing youth ministry.

The majority of youth pastors emphatically agree that denominational labels do not help them reach students with the Gospel – "in any way, shape or form." In a study of Kansas City demographics, the greatest church growth has come through independent, non-denominational churches from both the charismatic and non-charismatic persuasions.

The issue of waning denominational influence has worked its way into a frequently discussed topic that seems to manifest itself more openly all the time. Youth pastors who work within a strategic ministry network are apt to say, "I'm more excited about working with fellow youth pastors from other denominations to reach the students in our local high school than I am about driving across the state to a denominational conference." This is not a rebellious, disloyal attitude, but rather a purpose-driven, spirit-led desire to reach students for Jesus.

The YouthWorker Journal recently featured a special section called "*Seven Ministry Trends to Watch in the Next Decade*" One of the trends was, "*The*

Postdenominational Church." The signs point to the fact that denominations are...

> *Becoming less and less necessary. Though some will fight valiantly to save them, denominations are a dying breed. We're entering a postdenominational age. This is the wave of the future. We once rallied around denominations – those doctrinally similar to us – and more recently we've organized around large teaching churches. And now more than ever, Christians are connecting across denominational lines. And on this front of community, youth workers must lead the way. Let's face it: Many of our senior pastors are beholden to their denominations. They went to denominational seminaries, and denominations offer them financial and job security. It's going to be up to us – the youth workers – to take the courageous steps needed to reunify Christ's church. I say let's meet the challenge. We can take risks our bosses cannot. We can rally all the Christian churches of our communities for the one cause we all have in common. We always talk about 'one church.' We even sing about it. Now is our time to do something about it.* [4]

According to church growth expert Dr. Leith Anderson,

> *Denominational representation is a motivation not easily passed down to the next generation. They don't care as much. This attitude frustrates the founders who bemoan the decline of their church and the coming day when "there will no longer be a church of our denomination in this community."* [5]

Dr. Anderson is not alone. "The day of the denomination is not dead," says Elmer Towns, "but the new passion, is for *like ministry* as denominations change the way they play the game. The new day... emphasizes moving toward a community of churches that are of like function and ministry." [6]

The Reformation of Unity

There is a great deal of talk today about a *New Apostolic Reformation*, which is related to an emphasis on the individual priesthood of the believer but also to the role of an *apostle*. Within the dynamic forces for change, this component also relates to the emphasis of unity in the church, an important and major focus for the emerging youth ministry structure in the new millennium.

Ephesians 4 clearly states the absolutely crucial need for unity in the body for a properly functioning church.

> *Make every effort to keep the unity of the Spirit through the bond of peace. There is one body and one Spirit – just as you were called to one hope when you were called – one Lord, one faith, one baptism; one God and Father of all, who is over all and through all and in all. But to each one of us grace has been given as Christ apportioned it…*

> *It was he who gave some to be apostles, some to be prophets, some to be evangelists, and some to be pastors and teachers, to prepare God's people for works of service, so that the body of Christ may be built up until we all reach unity in the faith and in the knowledge of the Son of God and become mature, attaining to the whole measure of the fullness of Christ. Then we will no longer be infants, tossed back and forth by the waves, and blown here and there by every wind of teaching and by the cunning and craftiness of men in their deceitful scheming. Instead, speaking the truth in love, we will in all things grow up into him who is the Head, that is, Christ. From him the whole body, joined and held together by every supporting ligament, grows and builds itself up in love, as each part does its work.*
>
> *Ephesians 4:1-16*

The Apostle Paul describes the positions of apostle, prophet, evangelist, pastor, and teacher. The role of the prophet is to initiate accountability. The role of the evangelist is to initiate relationships with God. The role of the pastor is to initiate care. The role of the teacher is to initiate knowledge. **The role we tend to over look is the role of the apostle. The role of the apostle is to initiate structure.**

The developing role of the apostle or the apostolic function comes from within the concept of this New Apostolic Reformation and coincides with the concept of a *new emerging youth ministry model*. Reggie McNeal, in his new book *Revolution In Leadership: Training Apostles for Tomorrow's Church,* writes about the need for a new type of leadership that reflects the leadership style of the apostles in the first century church.

> *The new leadership called for... is described as apostolic leadership. In our day, an era that resembles in many remarkable ways the age of Christian beginnings, the same kind of leader is needed that the early church enjoyed. In short, we need apostolic leaders!*[7]

God is raising up individual men and women, groups of men and women, and organizations that are focusing on structure, enabling the Church to strategically work together in every city to reach that city for Christ.

prophet	initiates accountability
evangelist	initiates relationships with God
pastor	initiates care
teacher	initiates knowledge
apostle	initiates structure

MICROSOFT STRIKES APPLE ALLIANCE

> "Dominant Microsoft Corp. and struggling Apple Computer Inc. announced 'a broad product and technology development agreement...'"[1]

If Microsoft and Apple, who have, in the past, had a genuine and deep disdain for one another, can set differences aside for the purpose of making money, how much more should the Church of Jesus Christ be willing to focus on the core of what it believes to be most important? Our partnering is for eternal results.

CHAPTER 8

Strategic Partnerships
New, Real, and Impacting Ministry Relationships

"Let's see. You're working with 350 or so students, and I'm working with 300 or so students, so together that's around 650." Joey Butler, a youth pastor from a large area church, and I were discussing the ministry impact we were each having on the students in our suburban school district. When we considered that the secondary school population we'd been called to reach numbered 7000 students, we concluded that while we were *fulfilled*, we were not *content* with our results.

I remember Joey saying, "I could double the amount of students I work with, I could create a facilities problem for my church, everyone would talk about the great job I was doing. And yet, I still can't reach all 7000. And I can't get those *7000 students* out of my mind. I can't get them out of my heart. We have to work together and try something new." On that day we committed ourselves to finding a way to work together strategically. This same conversation has been experienced by dozens of other youth workers in the Kansas City area and by hundreds of thousands all across the country as well. The cry is "we've got to work together, the job is too big to accomplish alone."

In *The Coming Revolution in Youth Ministry*, Mark Senter put it bluntly.

> *The stage is set for the coming revolution in youth ministry. It must happen. A spiritual vacuum exists. Fewer than one in four public high schools have a Christian presence focused on their campuses. The most effective youth groups in the nation rescue only an average of nine converts each year. The student world is facing a spiritual crisis of gigantic proportions.* [2]

Shifting Paradigms

Take a moment and think about this: you're living in a ship's cabin. There is only a single porthole in this room with which to view the outside world. Now you certainly have different viewpoints within that lone window. You can look down and see the water – you can look up and see the sky. And you can probably see a good bit of the horizon. But the porthole remains the extent to which you can perceive the outside world. And it is that portal that forms, to a large extent, the decisions that you make.

We all live our lives in this proverbial cabin. Now we don't feel cooped up – and we certainly don't feel that our vision is impaired – there's plenty to see from just this one spot. But unfortunately, this leaves us out of touch with many of the dynamic factors shaping our personal world. Our "ship" could be lost at sea or perilously close to running aground without our ever knowing it.

This is why from time to time we have to break out of the cabin and go up on deck. It doesn't just change our viewpoint, it changes our whole outlook – our paradigm. But a paradigm is even more than an outlook – it is our own personal model of the world and how we instinctively believe that it works. We can truthfully say that we have a new paradigm when we begin to make decisions spontaneously based upon a new, broader outlook. And since we as humans are, to a large degree, what we believe, ultimately our paradigm can be defined as the way we subconsciously choose as individuals and organizations to live out our lives.

In his book *Paradigms*, Joel Barker points out that new paradigms are usually created by trying to deal with "unsolved problems laying on the shelf of the prevailing paradigm." [3] The problem that is *laying on the shelf* of traditional youth ministry is that we were not reaching enough students with a quality, culturally-relevant, relationship-based presentation of the Gospel. A thorough and honest examination of the effectiveness of our personal ministry in fulfilling the Great Commission causes us to see the big picture and brings us humbly to the point where we acknowledge the need to work together to get the job done.

The idea of partnerships – working together, teaming up or forming "strategic organizational alliances" – is on the cutting edge of our modern business environment. More than 20,000 alliances were formed worldwide during 1997-1998. [4]

If Microsoft and Apple, who have, in the past, had a genuine and deep disdain for one another, can set differences aside for the purpose of making money, how much more should the Church of Jesus Christ be willing to focus on the core of what it believes to be most important? Our partnering is for eternal results.

Defining Objectives

It is critical to define objectives that need to be met in the formation of a strategic partnership. In the business world, one of the leading criteria for forming an alliance or partnership is to "focus on selecting, building, and deploying only those capabilities that can truly drive the market." [5] All evangelicals agree that reaching non-believers with the Gospel is the top priority and is therefore a very good objective upon which to partner.

The guidelines listed below are borrowed from *Smart Alliances*.[6] I have also expanded these points with examples of how these objectives might fuel the emergence of strategic citywide youth ministry partnerships and alliances.

· **Risk Sharing**

No one entity (church or parachurch) can afford the risk of laying it all on the line to reach students in an entire city. By teaming up and combining resources the task is achievable and the risks lessened.

· **Economies of Scale**

By joining forces, we can combine human and financial resources and be more effective and efficient in getting the job done.

· **Technology Access**

Some groups face technology gaps in expertise or know-how. Partnerships can bring into the team people that possess the missing ingredients needed for success.

· **Geographic Access**

An individual church or ministry lacks the human resources to cover all the schools in their area, to reach all the students in a city. Working strategically together it can be done.

· **Handling Funding Constraints**

By working together, a citywide movement can gain momentum and capture the imagination of visionary people who will fund the mission.

Selecting Partners

Identifying and selecting strategic partners is the most crucial step in forming partnerships. For this to be successful you must first develop an effective process for screening and recruiting these partners. To assist us in selecting ministry partners, we established the following criteria:

- · Our partners must have a similar Mission.

- · Our partners must have ministry components that are compatible with our strategic plans, goals, and/or success criteria.

- · There must exist great potential for a win/win relationship within the prospective partnership.

- · The pursuit of our Vision must be enhanced by the partnership.

God's Command

If we are born of God we cannot be anything but part of the church, but we are never the whole. Even the local congregation is but a partial representation of the church, though it contains in its genes the DNA of its leader, the head of the church. We all belong to each other and we must act like that. An independent spirit is not a biblical option.
Paul McKaughan, President of Evangelical Fellowship of Mission Agencies [7]

Although we can go to our nearest bookstore or surf book sellers' web sites to peruse dozens of business titles on the "power of partnerships" or "how to form alliances," this concept is not a creation of modern business.

Luke records the success formula for working together strategically in the first century church in Acts 2:42-44:

> *They devoted themselves to the apostles' teaching and to the fellowship, to the breaking of bread and to prayer... everyone was filled with awe, and many wonders and miraculous signs were done by the apostles... [one of the main reasons for the power demonstrated by the early church is] all the believers were together.*

They were together. They were unified. They were, as Paul states in Philippians 1:27, "standing firm in one spirit, contending as one man for the faith of the Gospel." The resulting power of their unity is quickly revealed in Acts 2:47, "the Lord added daily those who were being saved." Out of this church came the strategy that "turned the world upside down" (Acts 17:6 KJV). What is emerging today within churches – specifically among youth pastors in cities all across our country – is a return to the first century church model found in the New Testament!

What is THE Church?

We know these groups of believers were meeting in many different homes and buildings in cities all over the Roman Empire. So how did Paul address Christians in each city in his letters? He referred to the "Church of God in Corinth" in I and II Corinthians 1:2. In Revelation, John referred to the "Church in Ephesus," the "Church in Smyrna," the "Church in Pergamum," and so forth. Paul did not start out the book of Thessalonians by addressing the individual house churches. Paul spoke to the Christians in the city collectively as the "Church of the Thessalonians."

God's heart is for the Church to be unified – unified to reach a city. God loves cities. He sent Jonah to Nineveh, Ezekiel was sent to Babylon, Paul was sent to Athens, Rome, and Philippi, etc. Could it be that, like the Church at the beginning of the first century, we sit at the dawn of the 21st century rediscovering God's formula for winning a city, a nation, a continent and ultimately the world?

In John 17:20-23, Jesus prayed,

> *My prayer is not for them alone. I pray also for those who will believe in me through their message, that all of them may be one, Father, just as you are in me and I am in you. May they also be in us so that the world may believe that you have sent me. I have given them the glory that you gave me, that they may be as one as we are one! I in them and you in me. May they be brought to complete unity to let the world know that you sent me and have loved them even as you have loved me.*

Why Now?

In Kansas City alone, approximately 200 youth workers have formed a partnership called the YouthFront Alliance. Over 300 churches participate in efforts to reach the secondary school students in the greater Kansas City area. Twenty networks of youth pastors are meeting regularly to work together in strategic, purpose-driven ministry efforts. We are no longer polarized into opposing factions – the church vs. the parachurch. We are together, unified in the Body of Christ.

I have already mentioned that a few youth workers had been networking for years in Kansas City. However, it wasn't until the Equal Access phenomenon kicked into high gear that the YouthFront Alliance came together in a strategic, citywide, multi-denominational way. The synergy is contagious. Youth workers are raving about the life-changing paradigm shifts they are making and the fulfillment they are experiencing from working together as the "Church of Kansas City." What really blows me away and keeps me awake at night is the exciting reality that what's happening in Kansas City is also appearing spontaneously and simultaneously across the country. Why is this?

Chapters six and seven listed a plethora of dynamic forces contributing to the emergence of a "citywide, focused, inter-denominational, church-centered, campus-based, purpose-driven, values-directed, strategy-oriented and unified movement." Here's a quick recap:

- Technology makes it possible to effectively communicate to the entire body, which is essential to a large, multi-faceted organizational structure.
- Professionally trained youth workers are realizing the importance of strategic, purpose-driven efforts.
- Students do not get hung up on denominational, sectarian labels or differences. They just naturally come together on campus as the Body of Christ.
- Churches and ministry organizations are reinventing how they lead and manage.
- The denominational influence and control on how a local church youth worker engages in ministry is declining.
- Christian students are coming together in unprecedented ways for ministry and prayer efforts.
- In the past, it was the parachurch youth worker that focused on the campus, but the church youth pastors of today have risen to the challenge of campus ministry.
- Our post-Christian culture, increasingly antagonistic to the truth and moral absolutes found in scripture, is an ominous reminder that youth workers must combine forces.

These are just some of the many changes in the air. Tie all the dynamics together with the theme of a Reformation of Unity, and it's no wonder that the soil is fertile for change – sweeping change.

The Senior Pastor

The senior pastor is a tremendous force in deciding how youth workers will engage in strategic ministry partnership. Unfortunately, there are occasions when a youth pastor is able to commit time, energy and resources to a strategic ministry partnership outside of their local church because the pastor is generally not interested in what his youth pastor is doing. Fortunately, this situation is ever decreasing. In fact, the new gen-

eration of pastors coming into the pulpits today is among the first generation of Christians who, in most cases, grew up as teenagers involved in a
church youth group with a professionally trained youth pastor. For them,
the importance of a dynamic youth ministry is not questioned.

In addition, a majority of new, young senior pastors have served as youth
workers in a church or parachurch setting. Their experience as youth pastors carries over to their new position. They tend to place a high priority
on a thriving youth ministry in their church. Lee Jost is a young man who
came to Christ through the ministry of his youth pastor here in Kansas
City. Now Lee serves as a youth pastor under his former youth pastor,
who is now the senior pastor. This example is not uncommon.

Youth Ministry – For Life?
There is a strong emphasis today on the validity of lifelong youth ministry.
More and more youth workers are pledging to do youth work until the
day they die. This mindset has had a positive effect on youth work and
has served to counteract and provide balance to the idea that youth ministry is something you do until you're ready to move on to bigger and better things. When a youth pastor is genuinely called by God to move into
the role of a senior pastor or some other church position, he or she often
has to deal with the lifelong youth ministry sentiment.

I have been in many a network meeting when one of our fellow youth
workers announced he was taking a senior pastor position. The
announcement is usually followed by joking harassment about "departing
the faith," "leaving the highest calling." Even though the kidding is in good
humor, you can usually tell that the individual really struggled with a sense
of violating some sacred pledge. The soon-to-be-former youth worker
usually concludes the announcement by saying he will always be a youth
pastor at heart and youth ministry will be a foundational priority of his
church.

It also seems that a high proportion of new, aggressive and entrepreneurial
senior pastors are coming to that position with a youth ministry para-

church background. Tom Nelson, an innovative pastor of the fast growing Christ Community Church in Overland Park, Kansas, is a former para-church youth worker. Tom feels that it is time for the church to employ the same creative entrepreneurial strategies that the successful parachurch ministries have used. Tom is a firm believer in the future of youth ministry strategic partnerships. It's exciting to see that there are more and more Tom Nelsons in church leadership today.

The bottom line is that more and more new pastors of this generation have a passion for youth ministry. In fact, in Kansas City we are finding that many senior pastors are so excited about the YouthFront Alliance of youth workers working together that they are incorporating involvement in the YouthFront Alliance networks and on-campus ministry into their youth pastors' job descriptions. In addition, more senior pastors today are involving us in their process to hire a youth pastor because they want a person who will get on board with what is happening here in Kansas City.

How do we create this kind of citywide, strategic partnership and teamwork? The answer is three-fold: by building structure, trust, and teamwork.

CHAPTER 9

Partnership Engineering
Structure, Trust and Teamwork –
Building Blocks to a Solid Partnership

Structure

It is not enough to just have an idea of what you want to accomplish in a youth ministry partnership. Every unified and organized ministry effort requires a well-defined Mission, Vision, Organizational Strategy, Doctrinal Statement and a Set of Values. This is of utmost importance for the initial building and ongoing well being of a strategic partnership.

Before we launched our Strategic Local Church Partnership, the YouthFront Alliance in Kansas City, we spent a great deal of time developing this structure. This meant spending a massive amount of time in writing, reassessing, editing, and re-writing these building blocks. But this process was an absolute necessity for the birth of a solid partnership. All tenets had to be carefully discussed and developed – and once agreed upon, they had to be (and must still be) consciously implemented and regarded each day.

Definitions

It may be helpful if we define some key terms at this point...

· Our Mission defines why a partnership exists.
  For example, the Mission Statement of the YouthFront Alliance is:
  Uniting the church to bring youth into a growing relationship with Jesus Christ.

- Our Vision describes the desired future destination of a partnership. For example, the Vision Statement of the YouthFront Alliance is: *To see that every secondary school student in the K.C. area hears the Gospel and gets connected to a church.*

- A Set of Values defines a partnership's culture. Here are a couple of examples...

  We will draw conclusions based on facts, not assumptions.

  We will respect each other's privacy, opinions, and beliefs.

  We will strongly consider the long-term implications of decisions.

- Doctrinal Statement This document describes the doctrinal beliefs of the partnership. You can view YouthFront's complete Doctrinal Statement in Appendix A.

While each entity within a partnership can and should have its guiding tenets, a unique Mission, Vision, Set of Values, and Doctrinal Statement that all partners can agree upon are the most crucial elements in the development of a citywide Strategic Local Church Partnership. Since these components drive a partnership's daily activities, they require an in-depth, focused process in order to be developed and refined.

Living the Values

The values that were established for the YouthFront Alliance created a foundation upon which youth workers could build trust and working relationships with each other. These values clearly spelled out how we would work together, what we would and would not do. But it was not just placed on paper and forgotten; only by living these values day to day, every day, can a solid structure of mutual trust and a spirit of unity be established. Chapter eleven provides an in-depth example of the values developed for the YouthFront Alliance *Project LEAP.*

Trust

Trust is built, not born. Trusting relationships among youth pastors should be developed around three basics:

1. Honesty

2. True concern for each other

3. Meaningful, candid, ongoing communication

These three basics create trust and with it, the powerful synergy necessary to capture a city for Christ. In our particular case, this trust moves the partnership forward to reach every student in every school. It is impor-tant that any partnership includes within its Set of Values some value statements that address the issue of trust.

Teamwork

The New Testament stresses *unity*. (As stated earlier, the power of the unified church turned the world upside down!) In his book, *The Fifth Discipline*, Peter Senge goes so far as to suggest this shared understanding – or unity – must be reinforced each day: "Building shared vision must be seen as a central element of the daily work of leaders. It is ongoing and never ending." [1]

Alignment is also a critical part of successful teamwork. Senge reminds us that a partnership is hardly a partnership if the participants are not aligned. Not only should they embrace the same vision, but also they must be able to *work together*.

> *The fundamental characteristic of the unaligned team is wasted energy. Individuals may work extraordinarily hard, but their efforts do not efficiently translate to team effort. By contrast, when a team becomes more aligned, a commonality of direction emerges, and individuals' energies harmonize.* [2]

This concept will hardly come as a surprise to anyone who has suffered through the tribulation of matching an organization's goals with the myriad of individual ideas and means to accomplish the goal: you feel like you're running in ten directions at once!

Senge offers these two drawings to illustrate this point.[3] The larger arrow is the partnership and the small arrows are the partners. You can easily imagine the unaligned team moving in an unpredictable fashion while the aligned team moves synergistically towards its goals and mission.

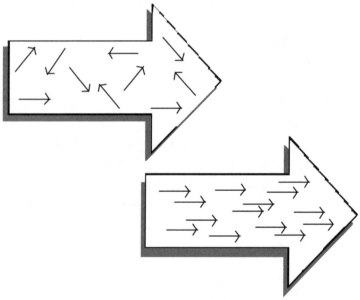

I particularly like the way Ken Blanchard states it:

> *Human energy is like the energy of light. When it is dissipated, as in the average light bulb, it gets work done in an average way. But when that same energy is focused and concentrated in a single direction, as with a laser beam, it has the power to cut through any kind of obstacle*[4]

Translation: Not even the gates of Hell will stand up to the power that will emerge when youth pastors in cities all over the world come together – unify – for the purpose of reaching every student in every school for Jesus

Christ. Or as I like to envision it: when a citywide, strategically focused youth ministry partnership is unified it meets the criteria for the unlimited power of the Holy Spirit to bring about supernatural results.

I recently attended a YouthFront Alliance network meeting. There were ten youth pastors in attendance from ten different local churches – but who collectively view themselves as one team. Their united goal is to reach the lost students from seven area secondary schools. I remember the intense emotion we felt as Doug Sword, a youth pastor from Cornerstone Church, choked back tears with these words:

> *Working together to reach the students in our city has shifted my focus beyond the four walls of my church and shown me that I have a ministry with a lot more students than those who attend my church. These students aren't my kids or your kids; they are our kids, God's kids.*

CHAPTER 10

Primed to LEAP
KCYFC Contemplates a New Future

Billions of stars twinkled brightly in the sky, unpolluted by the lights of any city. It was 2:00 a.m. and I was lying on my back in the middle of a paved country road with several fellow youth workers somewhere in the Ozark Mountains. We were on a staff getaway – a time to recharge, think and plan. At this particular moment we were caught up in God's awesome display of the infinite. How *big* God seemed. We were overwhelmed, boldly believing that with this God on our side, we could accomplish historic things. Even though we were serving together in a parachurch youth ministry oftentimes labeled "the world's largest local youth ministry," that night we all felt our mighty God could enable us to do so much more.

I remember saying, "Wouldn't it be awesome if we could develop a program for students on school campuses where we join forces with church youth pastors so we could reach every school in Kansas City?" The reaction of Jamie Roach (our future YouthFront Alliance Coordinator) was concise and immediate: "Let's do it." And we talked and dreamed late into the night…

Between 1984 and 1995, youth workers all over the country were having encounters like our Ozark experience. There would be many discussions, experiments and ideas on how to reach more students with the Gospel. Why? Because something new was happening in the U.S. – the Equal Access Act. This act promised to prevent discrimination against the religious speech of students in public schools and protect the rights of students to initiate student-led religious meetings on campus (if the school allows other non-curriculum clubs to meet on campus).

In 1984 the Equal Access Act was passed in the U.S. Senate, 88 to 11. It then passed in the House of Representatives by 337 to 77. Ronald Reagan signed it into law in August of that same year. But the Act in its original form pertained (or so it was construed) only to the college campus. The movement gained momentum in 1990 when the Supreme Court, through Westside Community Board of Education vs. Mergens, upheld, with an 8 to 1 decision, that the Act applied to the high school campus as well. Christian students were given the green light to form Christian clubs on campus. Unfortunately, it would be several years before the new freedoms this law provided would affect youth ministry strategies.

In May 1997, we learned about an organization in Birmingham, Alabama called First Priority that was successfully engaging networks of youth pastors in a focused, campus ministry strategy. Five of us flew from Kansas City to Birmingham to meet with its director, Todd Roberts. Several weeks later we met his twin brother, Mark Roberts. Mark had helped start the work in Birmingham and was now launching the strategy in Atlanta. It didn't take long for the Roberts brothers to sell us on the concept.

This encounter came at a great time for us because we had been moving away from a traditional youth ministry parachurch model to a Church Assisting Organization model. We had already shifted our focus to building youth pastor networks and were engaged in servant leadership to church youth workers. However, our networks lacked a focused purpose and enthusiasm.

As we've already mentioned, if a network of youth workers lacks purpose it will deteriorate. However, the same is true when only a short-term purpose exists. For example, if the network exists just to produce isolated events, motivation will eventually disappear. Isolated events misdirect and expend energy. Youth workers already have too much to do without adding another event. And if that event doesn't fit into a purpose-driven, grander scheme, it soon becomes a lot of work with little results.

Student-led Ministry

Today's students are willing to take the initiative to be missionaries to their public high school campuses. They alone have the platform to lead their generation to a life-changing personal commitment to Jesus Christ. They don't need us to get in their way. Rather, they need our prayers. They need our encouragement. They need our support and guidance. They need these things from us as they head to the front line each day to proclaim the Good News through their words and actions.

If you spend a good deal of time around teenagers, I'm sure you are as amazed as I am at the boldness and commitment of Christian students. These students are definitely not the church of tomorrow; they are the church of today! Nicki is one of these young people.

Nicki Brummett was one of 60 students on a mission team I led to Ireland. I will never forget Nicki's story of how God spoke to her while she was watching a herd of cows graze in a field.

> I watched these cows wander all the way to the other side of the field to eat grass when there was grass right under their feet. I'm so glad I came on this trip to Ireland. I wandered all the way here to do great things for God. But God has really spoken to me about reaching my own campus back home, where there is "grass" right under my own feet. You know what else? I had to raise the money to go to Ireland. But my government pays my way so I can spend nine months on the greatest mission field I have: my high school campus.

I wept.

Eight months later, after launching our campus strategy through the YouthFront Alliance, I had the opportunity to present the Good News of Salvation through Jesus at Nicki's school club. Nicki and 100 of her peers were there when twelve of her friends asked Christ into their lives. After the meeting I was talking to the student leaders when one piped up, "Can you believe twelve of our friends got saved?" Nicki replied in a hushed tone, "I can. We have been praying and fasting for God to work." I know Nicki Brummett. She wasn't using the statement to proclaim how spiritual she was. Her statement was a pure, innocent response to the question. Once again Nicki had brought me to tears.

I have never gotten used to a student's profound demonstration of faith or seeing a student's life changed by Jesus. What could be more rewarding than giving your life to seeing students changed by the Gospel?

SECTION 4

The LEAP

> "That's one small step for man...
> One giant LEAP for mankind..."
>
> *Neil Armstrong, 1st ever moon landing*

CHAPTER 11

Taking the LEAP
KCYFC Moves Forward

The LEAP Equation:
Linking + Evangelism + Access = Power

After developing an extensive plan, replete with Mission statements, Values, and a business plan, KCYFC took the LEAP – a strategy for reaching youth in the 21st century. LEAP is not an organization; rather, it is a *concept* to unite local church youth leaders into a network of support for student-led evangelistic campus clubs. I believe this concept will serve as the stimulus for creating a citywide youth ministry as we enter a new millennium. Once the catalyst of a citywide co-operative LEAP concept is established, a genuine paradigm-shift will emerge. We will no longer be bound by the old patterns of church vs. parachurch. There will be one whole, unified Church working together to reach students.

Here is a brief idea of how the LEAP Equation works:

Linking
If we want to see this generation of young people won to Christ, we have no choice but to work together. Youth workers must unite around the essentials of the Christian faith. Everyone must agree: "No logos, no egos." We join hands – link together – for the greater cause of Christ, knowing from scripture that together we can accomplish what none of us can do alone.

Evangelism

Evangelism gives direction and focus to the LEAP equation. We all acknowledge that prayer and Bible study are essential for Christian growth. But these are not the end-purposes of a LEAP-modeled organization. Everyone should understand first and foremost that this strategy is for the purpose of winning young people to Jesus Christ.

Access

Access to the social center of youth was a missing component for years. But praise God, He has, through the Federal Equal Access Act, changed everything. Now students have the access they need on their school campus to live out their faith. Christian students can fellowship together, Christian students can work together, and Christian students can use this newfound access to tell their friends about the life-changing work of Christ in their lives.

Power

Do you want to see your city radically changed? Are you ready to see youth come to Christ by the hundreds – the thousands? When you put the previous three components together, the result is the fourth – POWER. The power to change lives. The power to change the world. It's the power of God – and it's being unleashed across the nation as this strategy takes hold.

Remember, it's an equation

$$L + E + A = P... \text{ LEAP!}$$

Get Ready to LEAP on Your Own

The YouthFront Alliance on-campus club is called Club121. Its focus is one-to-one evangelism. Other cities use First Priority, Youth Alive, etc. However, we believe that it is important for every city to take this concept and develop their own name for the sake of local ownership and control. The following chapter will help you get started.

CHAPTER 12

Values-Based Partnerships
Doing Ministry Business Using Biblical Principals

Chapter nine introduced the importance of creating a Doctrinal Statement and a Set of Values that all partners can agree on. They are, perhaps, the most crucial elements in the development of a citywide strategic partnership of youth pastors. In particular, the importance of *values* cannot be understated. Shared values, as we discussed earlier, keep those in and around the partnership working in harmony to fulfill the mission.

LEAP's strategic partnership values contain distinctive and core beliefs that define the culture of the organization. I hope you will use the following points to springboard a discussion that helps your citywide partnership define its own Set of Values.

LEAP Values

1. **A Youth Worker Strategic Partnership Must Be Church-Focused.**
   If the network does not center on the support and involvement of the local churches in your area, your venture is destined for failure. The old model – a disunited (sometimes even hostile) relationship betwee parachurch and church – is outdated. The LEAP model requires a different kind of parachurch entity (a Church Assisting Organization), one whose life and vitality is derived from the impassioned involvement of the local church.

2. **Strategic Youth Ministry Partnership Must Be Campus-Centered.**
   The life of every 21st century teenager takes place, almost exclusively, on the school campus. We could wish this wasn't the case, but we have to come to terms with the reality. Our Strategic Local Church

Partnership and the churches it represents must realize that to reach teenagers, we must go to where they are. Jesus never told his disciples that the lost would seek Him out – rather, He stated, "I have come to *seek* and to save that which was lost... "We must follow Christ's example.

3. A Youth Worker Strategic Partnership Must Be Built Upon Common Beliefs Shared by All Evangelicals.
(see Doctrinal Statement in Appendix A)
All evangelicals agree that young people today need Jesus. While individuals may disagree on issues that are specific to a denomination, everyone involved in the Strategic Local Church Partnership must agree that when working together we will look past these particulars toward the greater cause of Christ. We cannot allow a strong personality or a singular local church to hijack this value. If everyone in the Strategic Local Church Partnership cannot agree on this premise, we must seek out more mature personalities in order to see the LEAP concept go forward in our cities. A youth worker Strategic Local Church Partnership must be an interdenominational ministry and its programs must never be used to promote, practice, or criticize beliefs that are unique to some but not necessarily common to all evangelicals.

4. A Youth Worker Strategic Partnership Is Not a Platform for Members to Promote Individual Programs to Students.
Only Strategic Local Church Partnership sponsored events should be advertised through student meetings and/or publications. This builds trust between partnership members and insures that conflicts do not arise between local churches within the partnership. While partnership members may be tempted to slip in a little information to students regarding a function with their individual church, this action must be seen as subversive to the whole and dealt with immediately. Following this course will ensure a good working environment and is a big step toward a mature citywide youth worker partnership.

5. **Youth Worker Strategic Partnership Members Must Be Supportive and Non-critical of Other Members and Other Youth Ministries.**

There is no place within your Youth Worker Partnership for members to sit in judgement over each other – or over any other ministry that is building the Kingdom. While it is important that any person or ministry pass through the sieve of basic sound doctrine *(see Doctrinal Statement in Appendix A)*, we must strive constantly to be non-critical toward other ministry workers and methods – even though they may be radically different from ours. On the contrary, youth worker partnership members should go out of their way to encourage and uplift each other and the members of other ministries.

6. **Youth Workers are Stewards, Not Owners of Students.**

Students belong to the Lord. Youth workers have the awesome responsibility of working with the students entrusted to them. While this concept is easy to acknowledge on paper, it is difficult to live out. We must have faith that God is sovereign – that His work will be accomplished in the life of a student regardless of whether or not it is through us personally that He chooses to work. We must be faithful to God when He assigns a student to us, have faith in God when he chooses someone else, and ask God for wisdom to know the difference between the two.

7. **Students Must Have Ownership of their On-Campus Evangelistic Clubs.**

It is essential, both for students' morale and for legal concerns, that each Equal Access Club be initiated and led by students. Student leadership and involvement is the number one key to establishing and maintaining effective on-campus clubs. We also must be vigilant to live by the letter and spirit of the Equal Access Act. While youth workers can and must be very intentional about coaching students in methods and strategy, it is ultimately the students that must do the work of launching and administrating each Club.

8. An On-Campus Evangelistic Club Should Include Students from as Many Denominations as Possible.
   There is strength in numbers. Just as we work together in harmony with our Youth Worker Partnership, we must motivate students to work with any and all Christian students on campus. We must teach students how to minimize their differences in order to maximize their impact. Jesus prayed, "that all of them may be one, Father, just as you are in me and I am in you." As Jesus modeled this precept for us, we must model it to the next generation. Only through the *combined* efforts of every Christian student on campus will the LEAP strategy work at its maximum potential.

9. The Gospel Presentation Must Never Be Compromised.
   The Gospel must always be presented clearly and with the utmost integrity. "I am not ashamed of the Gospel, because it is the power of God for the salvation of everyone who believes" (Romans 1:16). The Gospel message should never be unclear about man's sin nature or God's redeeming power through the death of His one and only son, Jesus Christ. It is the simple Gospel message that changes lives.

10. **The Gospel Presentation Must Always Be Presented in a Way That is Relevant to Current Youth Culture.**
    Jesus went to great lengths to put His message into language that the people of His day could understand. He wanted people to be able to relate to the Kingdom of Heaven on a very practical level. We should strive to do the same. Plan and labor painstakingly on new and creative ways to tell the Gospel story without sounding like yesterday's news. The Gospel is alive! So don't let its presentation be dead! We must diligently work with other Youth Worker Partnership members to ensure that we challenge students to be fresh and current in the methods through which the Gospel story is told.

11. **A Christian Student's Life Must Include Integrity Friendships with Non-believing Peers.**

Christian students have a responsibility to show their non-Christian peers the difference that Christ makes in their everyday lives. Many Christian young people retreat into a safe circle of friends, all of whom are believers. We must challenge students to move out of their comfort zone and into the lost and hurting world that surrounds them daily. This can be frightening. The best way to teach a student this value is to live it out in our own lives.

12. **A Young Person's Christian Growth Must Include Involvement in a Local Evangelical Church.**

Involvement with an Equal Access Club on campus should never replace a student's involvement in the local church. Church life is essential for a student's discipleship, training, nurturing, and fellowship. While there will naturally be growth that occurs from participation with an on-campus club, we must never mistake this for the kind of growth necessary to develop a student into a mature believer. Youth workers and Christian students must be diligent to connect new believers to a local church body where they can be discipled to be followers of Jesus.

13. **Youth Workers Must Live a Life of Personal Integrity, Fully Devoted to Jesus Christ.**

The Epistles are filled with instructions on how we are to lead by example. The older are to instruct, the younger, for example. We must be above reproach in our lives. We must be more concerned about *being* than d*oing.* A life of seeking the face of God is what we owe the students to whom we minister.

14. **Youth Workers Can Maximize Their Impact on Youth by Working Together.**

"May the God who gives endurance and encouragement give you a spirit of unity among yourselves as you follow Christ Jesus, so that with one heart and mouth you may glorify the God and Father of our

Lord Jesus Christ" (Romans 15:5,6). Since it is in the heart of God for us to work together in unity, we know that working together will bring greater results. Working together in a citywide Strategic Local Church Partnership is not only more effective in reaching youth, it is also more fulfilling.

Immediate Results of a Values-Based Organization

Once all the organizational components were put in place, the YouthFront Alliance and Club121 took off. In a little more than a year we went from 40 youth pastors involved in four networks, to well over 200 youth pastors involved in the 20 YouthFront Alliance networks. Every YouthFront Alliance network has a representative youth pastor who serves on the (citywide) Advisory Team to help give leadership and input to the citywide effort of the YouthFront Alliance. Coached by these local church youth pastors, students now lead over 100 Club121s. In just the first six months of 1999, over 1500 students accepted Christ in recorded meetings alone. Due of the emphasis we place on relationship evangelism, the exact count of salvation decisions is unknown. Within a five-month period of that same year, we held two citywide YouthFront Alliance/Club121 events with a combined total of nearly 15,000 in attendance. Over 600 students came to Christ at these events. The momentum of this citywide Strategic Local Church Partnership is just now picking up steam, and the youth pastors in Kansas City are dreaming bigger dreams.

A New Dynamic Emerges: <u>One Church</u> in Kansas City

One of the most exciting developments has been the subtle shift away from the on-campus club as the primary reason we work together toward a new focus on the biblical command to work together as the Church in Kansas City. What started out as a network of youth pastors to facilitate on-campus evangelistic clubs is becoming the citywide Youth Church of Kansas City working to fulfill multiple purposes of The Church.

· In one Advisory Team meeting, several youth pastors suggested starting a Praise Night for those students involved in Club121.

It launched successfully. What a sight it is to see hundreds of students and dozens of youth pastors consumed by God through worship. The format is simple, but the results are profound when students from all over our city come together to sing praises to God, testify to what God is doing in their lives, read scripture, and pray.

· Youth pastors in several of the YouthFront Alliance networks are discussing a citywide student mission program based on Acts 1:8; Jerusalem, Judea, Samaria, and the uttermost parts of the world.

· The YouthFront Alliance youth pastors are engaging their students in local (Jerusalem) missions projects.

· The YouthFront Alliance networks are discussing a partnership of suburban and urban students to make a stronger impact on our city.

· International mission trips organized around networks and/or schools are beginning.

· A village outside of Monterrey, Mexico has been adopted. and dozens of Kansas City youth groups will cover ten weeks of ministry there during the summer.

· 1500 students are coming together for Serve Day, a citywide work project in the urban core of Kansas City.

· Over 15,000 students are coming together for Millennial Meltdown, a citywide Club121 evangelistic event.

The camaraderie and friendships that have developed among youth pastors involved in the YouthFront Alliance has been amazing. Several youth pastors have confided in us that their involvement in the YouthFront

Alliance and Club121 has been a factor in deciding to continue in their present position. We believe that youth pastors connected in partnership with other youth pastors will add to youth ministry longevity.

A Network in Action

Let me share an example how a network of youth pastors works to facilitate innovative youth ministry.

In Blue Springs, the Kansas City suburb where I live, there are seven secondary schools and approximately 7000 students. Our youth pastors' network meets for two hours every other week. In each of our churches we have students that attend all of the different schools. There is no way one youth pastor could work on campus with all his/her students attending the various schools, so we divided the schools among us. Through our church events and programs, we promote the on-campus club to our students. Each youth pastor has a Student Leadership Team comprised of students from different churches who attend their focus school. We coach the students in our school to lead their on-campus club. Periodically, we bring the students together to show them that they are not alone but part of a movement. We discuss our goal for our students to identify with two youth pastors, one at church and one at school.

Our flock has enlarged. We no longer only look out for the kids in our youth group but watch all the students that God has allowed our network to work with. Over 1000 students are involved with the on-campus ministry in Blue Springs alone. We are definitely having fun.

> " These who have turned the world
> upside down have come here too. "
>
> *Acts 17:6*

CHAPTER 13

The ACTS Revolution

Equipping Students to be Missionaries on Their
High School Campuses

Once the LEAP concept was formulated, we knew it was time to create the on-campus clubs. This too needed a solid structure. After all, this is where the action would be! We worked with First Priority of America to design a strategy for on-campus clubs. This template, which guides the students in how to use their on-campus evangelistic club, is called The ACTS Revolution. The ACTS is an acronym based on a four-week cycle: A, C, T, and S.

Accountability Week

The A in ACTS stands for *Accountability Week*. During this campus meeting the students hold each other accountable to how they are doing in their walk with Christ. They inquire of each other on how they are doing with their witness to lost friends. They encourage each other to be praying for and inviting their lost friends to Seek Week.

Challenge Week

The C in ACTS stands for *Challenge Week*. During this meeting the students invite a youth pastor or other special guest to present a challenge to the students. This week focuses on challenging students to be a bold witness, take a stand for Christ and be the salt and light for Christ on campus.

Testimony Week

The T in ACTS stands for *Testimony Week*. During this week, students share testimonies of what Christ is doing in their lives and how he is using them to reach their friends for Jesus.

Seek Week

The S in ACTS stands for *Seek Week* Seek Week is when the Christian students invite their non-believing friends to come so they can be exposed to the Good News.

After Seek Week, the revolution begins again with Accountability Week, where new Christians can be encouraged and checked up on.

Living the Book of Acts

The ACTS Revolution provides direction for students from multiple denominations to work together to reach their school for Christ. This is an on-campus revolution led by students and modeled after the book of Acts.

We read in the book of Acts that people were being added daily to the church. This seems to be happening in Kansas City also. Rarely does a day go by without another victory report of students accepting Christ on campus. Recently, twelve students gave their lives to Jesus in the first Seek Week of a new Club121. Two days later, two middle school Club121s joined together for an evening outreach. Over 200 students came. One youth pastor played in the band and another presented the Gospel. Before the night was over, 68 students had prayed to receive Christ as their Lord and Savior. WOW!

Another exciting dynamic of a citywide Strategic Local Church Partnership is the natural infrastructure that can follow up on new believers. Effective follow-up has always been a special challenge for traditional youth ministry parachurch organizations because the local church is best equipped to disciple a new believer. The benefit of a structured, strategic partnership among local churches is the infrastructure that is in place to get students connected.

Perhaps this e-mail from one of our YouthFront Area Coordinators best illustrates what is happening. It may be a bit long, but every word is telling:

I recently attended Seek Week at Lake View Middle School. Jeremy Rezen shared the Gospel and 5 students prayed to receive Christ. Daniel Morris, the Campus Coach and youth pastor of 1st Baptist Church of North Kansas City, immediately took the Seek Week response cards and began to follow up on the salvation decisions. Daniel wrote notes to each of the students who prayed to receive Christ, and also sent them a "Jump Start" book. One of the students had stated on his card that he occasionally attended Tiffany Fellowship Assembly of God. Daniel took the time to call Barry Young, the youth pastor at Tiffany Fellowship, and let him know that one of his "fringe" students had prayed to receive Christ at Club121, and then proceeded to give Barry the student's contact information.

Barry was taken back. He told me during a phone conversation that this one call concerning the student in his ministry did more than anything else to validate the ministry of Club121. At the time, Barry was a new youth pastor in town, and had not even been to a Club121 or the YouthFront Alliance meeting. He went on to state how impressed he was with the ministry of Club121.

Immediately Barry made contact with the student and started working on getting him plugged into Tiffany Fellowship's youth ministry on a regular basis. The value of effective follow-up is immeasurable. It both connects students to a local church ministry, but also can serve to connect youth workers to the ministry of Club121. Today I am picking up Barry and taking him to our YouthFront

Alliance network meeting where he will have a
chance to meet Daniel Morris and other Campus
Coaches/youth pastors in his area for the
first time.

Lee

YouthFront Area Coordinator

It's working! It's awesome! In 25 years of youth ministry I have never been so fulfilled as I am now, working with a Strategic Local Church Partnership to reach the students in our city for Jesus. Even more exciting news: what's happening in Kansas City is also happening, to some degree or another, simultaneously – and spontaneously – in cities across America such as Minneapolis/St. Paul, Portland, Dallas, Buffalo, Anchorage, Chattanooga, Washington, DC, Phoenix, Birmingham, and Atlanta.

This is an emerging movement birthed by God. I believe it will change how we do youth ministry as we enter a new millennium. Perhaps the only thing that will hinder this emerging movement could be our reluctance to change, or even more so, our limited efforts to seek the face of God and pray, "Thy Kingdom come."

> " We have not been called to simply maintain the aquarium, we have been called to be fishers of men. "
>
> *Ronnie Metsker*

CHAPTER 14

A Challenge to Church Youth Pastors

I doubt if there has a been a youth worker who has ever lived who didn't have some of these thoughts;

- "I know the youth group at *Having Too Much Fun Across the Street Church* has some exciting programs, but we are spiritually deeper and more relational."

- "If my kids go to the special event at that *1st Church of the Too Much Money with Nothing but Christian Rock Musicians to Spend it On* then they might get recruited away from my church."

- "I'm not going to promote that *Think They're Going to Win the World Campus Club* to my students. After all, I didn't have anything to do with organizing it."

- "If the *Chilling With My Kids Without My Permission Coffee House* is so cool, we'll start our own coffee house and do it better. Where's my coffee grinder?!"

These are my kids!!!

While these thoughts and thoughts like them may be common, they are not Kingdom thoughts. Think how much misdirected time and energy are spent on the above thoughts. For the sake of Christ and the students we profess to love so deeply, we must bring every self-centered thought into captivity. "We demolish arguments and every pretension that sets itself up against the knowledge of God, and we take captive every thought to make it obedient to Christ" (II Corinthians 10:5).

We must learn to embrace a stewardship instead of an ownership of the students entrusted to us. This is imperative to their long-term development.

This stewardship mindset only comes as we seek the face of God and see the big picture that these are God's kids, not ours.

Who Are These Kids?

According to the U.S. Census Bureau, there are 70 million people under the age of 18 in the United States alone. Elizabeth Large, a journalist for the *Baltimore Sun*, gives a broader perspective:

> *There are [now] more Millennials than there were Baby Boomers at their peak... The teenagers of this generation hate the idea of being lumped together. Kids born after 1979 live on the Internet or risk death snowboarding. They listen to 'N Sync, or maybe the Beatles. They wear cargo pants or dress like disco queens. They think the world is worth saving or they don't care that the hole in the ozone layer is growing and the Third World is getting poorer. One big difference between the two generations is that Baby Boomers were a relatively homogenous group, while the under-18s are ethnically very diverse.* [1]

The bottom line: there are enough kids and non-targeted people groups within the student population to keep us all professionally secure in youth ministry. Notice that this is *professional* security not *job* security. Often our insecurities in youth ministries come from the environment we are working in. Many churches talk about innovation but act like their primary mission is to maintain the status quo.

Attract New Believers Rather than Catering to Transfers

In *The New Reformation*, Lyle Schaller looks at this dilemma. He observes the typical *shrinking* congregation's focus to be on "the product" whereas the typical *growing* church is more likely to begin by identifying the needs of the unchurched. But what should be the number one factor in how we design our ministries, arrange our schedules, project expectations of our staff, and establish our priorities? Is it...

> · to take better care of our current members and to perpetuate local traditions?

> · to be sensitive and responsive to religious and personal needs of people we seek to reach with good news of Jesus Christ, but we have yet to meet? [2]

I think we can do both: meet the needs of our current students and reach non-believing students. Schaller states: "Perhaps the most subtle of these signs of hope is in the increasing number of congregations who conceptualize 'membership,' not as a destination but rather as a doorway into learning that leads to discipleship and subsequent involvement in doing ministry." [3]

To accomplish this requires one of the greatest paradigm shifts in the church today. We must move from an inward focus to an outward focus. The exciting thing is that it is happening.

Set Your Compass True North

When Bo Boshears and Troy Murphy from Willow Creek continually sang the song, "Be a youth ministry instead of a youth group," the message was a challenge to be outward-focused. To be inwardly focused makes our churches, our students, and ourselves spiritually retarded. Stephen Macchia, in his book, *Becoming a Healthy Church*, lists an outward focus as one of the ten characteristics of a healthy church. He also listed networking with the Body of Christ as a healthy characteristic. [4]

The strategy of *inwardly focusing* on teaching and training Christians students in our churches in order to prepare them for ministry "when they grow up" is not a healthy philosophy. And yet this thinking is thick in many congregations. How often do we hear, "Young people are the church of tomorrow." If you react strongly to that statement, good! Christian students are not the church of tomorrow; they are the church of today! In fact, I will stick my neck out to say those Christian students of this generation who hold an outward focus have much to teach the rest of the church about frontline ministry.

George Barna states it succinctly:

> *These days, teenagers struggle to identify the value of a church. They do not view churches to be productive, insightful, or comforting. They rarely find churches to be places that dispense wisdom, provide constructive development, facilitate meaningful relationships or provide public service. They view churches as antiquated organizations designed to promulgate "religious stuff" and to "live apart from the world instead of getting involved in the pain of the world."* [5]

Moreover, and to their credit, 6 out of 10 teenagers are more focused on God than on the institutional church. [6]

Our churches and youth ministries will be more relevant, effective and efficient if we focus outwardly on ministry to non-believers and disciple our Christian students in the midst of that process. When we challenge our students – those whom God has given us – to have an outward focus and be salt and light, we not only can disciple them effectively, but we can also reach non-believing students in a culturally relevant way at the same time.

The church, which is God's ordained institution, is the primary vehicle to reach the world. We must turn around the perception of church. We cannot afford to have the church perceived as culturally irrelevant. The church – along with the family – should be a constant in our lives from our first breath until our last. Chicago youth pastor, Harvey Carey, is convinced, "The church has a timeless, endless message to share Jesus Christ as our only mediator to God. However, many churches are using 8-track methods in a CD generation. The message doesn't have to change but the church must develop creative, innovative new methods."[7] Perhaps it's more telling to realize that many churches and ministry organizations that pride themselves as part of the CD generation are unaware that new, low-bandwidth computer file formats are really the cutting edge of recording technology today. **CHANGE HAPPENS.**

If we have an ownership mentality that tries to protect our students and keep them into "our thing," we actually reduce growth and potentially drive the students away. Dr. Leith Anderson states, "It is ironic that some of the most denominational churches least perpetuate the denomination, while some of the least denominational churches most perpetuate the denomination."[8]

Students are perceptive. They will go where their needs are being met. And one of their needs is to be a part of something that has *life*. How much life can our youth ministries have if we are inwardly focused or limited to a ministry within the group? If we could make a paradigm shift and spend more time focusing on making a bigger pie instead of spending time and energy worrying about our individual piece of the pie, we would all be better off.

"I'm Here to Invite Outsiders, Not Coddle Insiders"

The above quote is paraphrased from Matthew 9:12-13 in *The Message*. Unfortunately, this is all too true of many youth ministries who, as Doug Fields explains, "do an excellent job of coddling insiders but a lousy job of reaching the lost."[9]

Innovative pastor and church growth specialist Dr. Leith Anderson explains it this way:

> Churches that give away blessings are much more likely to be blessed. They are focused on others rather than themselves, open to outsiders with their new ideas and ways, inclusive rather than exclusive, outreaching rather than

> fortifying. These churches are for the twenty-first century. It is never an
> easy decision to be a blessing to outsiders. Nor is outreach painlessly imple-
> mented. When an inward church decides to give birth to an outward orien-
> tation, there will be pain. Some people will misunderstand. Anger may
> flare. A few might leave the church. Certainly the problems should not be
> sought, but they shouldn't be avoided either. [10]

When you focus on coddling insiders, your long-term results will be infe-
rior. Not only will you fail to reach outsiders, but the spiritual development of insiders will suffer as well.

That None Should Perish should be required reading for everyone in voca-
tional ministry. In it, Ed Silvoso makes this point:

> I know of no church that criticizes its pastor for not taking care of the needs
> of the lost sheep (salvation) but know of too many churches that have fired
> their pastors for not taking care of the 99 sheep that are safely tucked into
> the fold. Nothing could be more opposed to Jesus' teaching about the role of
> the pastor. In Luke 15:1-7, He emphasizes how the good shepherd leaves
> the saved sheep to go after the lost one. Our selfish preoccupation with our
> cosmetic needs at the expense of the eternal life of the lost is the ultimate
> expression of the religious spirit that controls many Christians today. Jesus
> loved sinners. He came to earth not because this was a holy place, but
> because it was populated exclusively by sinners. [11]

Passionate Leadership

When engaging in an outward-focused ministry of discipleship and
equipping students to reach their peers, we must be diligent about leadership. To be effective in life-changing youth ministry today takes more than
simply a good communicator who understands kids. We must take our
calling seriously. We must be strategic thinkers driven by mission and
vision. We must be oriented to the big picture. We must commit to
becoming consistent *learners*. This is *passionate leadership* and is the key to
strategic ministry.

We also need youth pastors who are more concerned about who they are
(being) instead of what they do (doing). By its nature, youth ministry is

very doing oriented. Our impact will be far greater if we nurture our personal walk with God and spend time being by praying, thinking, reflecting and strategizing. Remember, there are only so many hours in the day, so we must make sure what we choose to do is high leverage. The need is greater than ever, and the challenge can be overwhelming.

In many cities across the country youth workers are leading the way in pioneering Strategic Local Church Partnerships. The rest of the church is beginning to acknowledge what youth workers are doing together and are beginning to explore ways that other components of the church can partner to increase citywide effectiveness as "The Church of [Our City]."

Before we youth workers sprain our wrists patting ourselves on the back for our pioneering and cutting edge partnerships, may I remind each of us that up to now we have done this reactively. It would be nice to believe that we *proactively* partnered together to facilitate the birth of a new student movement. But it is the students who have led the way, under the direction of the Holy Spirit. It is their leadership, evidenced by such things as See You at the Pole and the Equal Access Club phenomenon, that has pulled us into networking to help facilitate these student-led efforts. *And a child shall lead them...*

I am hopeful that now with the citywide partnerships of youth pastors being formed across the country, we can be more intentional in growing these partnerships. We can turn our attention to implementing new cutting edge strategies to mobilize Christian students to reach the entire student population of a city with the Good News of Jesus Christ. "Let your light shine before men, that they may see your good deeds and praise your father in heaven" (Matthew 5:13-16). The time is right. The time is now!

Community Involvement

We are called to be a positive influence in our culture. Let's face it: for much of the last quarter century we have not excelled at making a difference. There were, of course, some political dynamics at work that resulted in the ineptness of the church. For example, our government's message that we had no right to enter the public domain with our biblical views and practices was a factor. Another factor has been the response of many Christians to pull out of popular culture, since we're not welcomed. Another dynamic was the preoccupation to change government through an orchestrated effort to elect Christian candidates. Unfortunately, our results were, in most cases, counter-productive.

"John Dewey, the principal architect of public education in 20th century America, argued that schools should erase the 'irrational religious influence of parents on their children.'" [12] "Unfortunately, many educators have embraced Dewey's anti-religious bias and do not see the church as a potential and positive ally. But Dewey's moment may be passing. Mounting failures in student discipline and academic performance are leaving school administrators hungry for new approaches. In surprisingly large numbers, schools are inviting religious groups back into the classroom. Asked to serve as tutors and aides, church volunteers are bringing with them their faith and the value system it inspires." [13]

A whole new generation of youth workers – one that understands the importance of building relationships with school administrators – is now on the scene. We've learned that instead of just cursing the darkness, it is so much more effective to light a candle. As we work with students to make an impact on their mission field (the school), we need wisdom so that instead of being an aggravation to the school administration, we can be a blessing. John Cutshall says,

> *For centuries Christians influenced music, art, government, and communities – until the mid 1900s, when something changed. For many reasons the church was told to take a back seat, and we obeyed, we lost much of our influence in the arts, literature, government, schools, and our communities. The good news is that the winds have changed, and once again people are looking to the church as an agent of influence in our communities.* [14]

Casting the Vision

Christian students are coming together on the campuses of their public schools to pray together and work together. We must encourage, equip, and empower these students to reach their non-believing friends: this is at the core in developing an outward-focused youth ministry. We must do all we can to help them succeed. This is their ministry, not ours. Are you ready to start?

Catching the Vision

One of our roles as a youth ministry leader is to constantly cast the vision of our ministry efforts. We must help those in the church – from the pastor and other church leadership to the parents and students – to see that the school campus is the primary youth ministry mission field. For example,

- Have students invite your pastor to speak at the on-campus club you work with.

- Take your church's key leaders to observe See You at the Pole.

- Have one of your student leaders go to the deacons or elders meeting and give a report of what is happening with campus ministry.

- Show the *Generations* video (*Mars Hill Productions*) series to your church's leadership.

- Expose your church to the on-campus ministry of your students.

- Systematically arrange for adults in your church to observe your students engaged in ministry.

The Missions Budget

The greatest single thing that can happen for your campus ministry is for local church leaders to see public school campuses as part of the church's overall missions strategy. When schools are classified as mission fields, doors open and resources appear. The responsibility for campus ministry is shared and no longer solely on your shoulder. [15]

Monty Hipp

"No matter how well-funded your youth ministry is, ask for money from your church's missions budget," cries Hipp. [16] Since a strong majority of those who become Christians do so before their 20th birthday, teen evangelism is a great investment.

Only a small number of adults still attend the church they grew up in. This is especially true in the mobile society in which we live. Look around at adults that attend your church. How many attended when they were teenagers? In some churches it's at 5%, or less. In most churches 10% would be a very high percentage. (Can you see why trying to "own" the students in your church youth group is ridiculous?) This quiet change in our church culture supports the premise that teen evangelism belongs in the mission budget. We are reaching and discipling students who will not be, for the most part, a member of our church as an adult. This is not a depressing fact. Let it excite you: our work is a true missions endeavor.

Teaming Up

Before you aggressively solicit mission funds from your church or go through the process of shifting your youth ministry's focus to an outward focus, make sure you build support with key influencers in your church. Greg Lafferty writes, "In church leadership, the Lord rarely works through lone individuals. Teamwork is the rule. If key leaders, advisors, parents, and volunteers get on board, there's a strong possibility the Lord is in the change." [17]

Mark Cannister, youth pastor at Emerson Park Church, stresses the need to bring about change and implement innovation through communication and constantly casting the vision to those around you: "Developing a strategic plan of innovation should not be done by the youth minister behind closed doors." [18]

To be effective in building support for your innovative efforts, you must have the right balance of humility and confidence in your direction. Humility comes from knowing that you are not the answer for saving the world, you're just a tool in God's hand. Confidence comes from knowing that God is not willing that any should perish. And He wants to use you to bring the students entrusted to you into a mature growing relationship with Jesus. It's humbling to believe that not only could God use you to effectively train students in your church, but He will also mobilize students and youth pastors from other churches to win your city to Christ.

Ed Silvoso writes,

> All the congregations in the city must realize that, biblically speaking, there is only one Church in the city. It is a church that meets in many congregations, but it is still one church. Although many under-shepherds are watching over those congregations, only one Chief Shepherd watches over the Church.[19]

What an exciting time to be involved in youth ministry. More and more resources are available, more students are accepting ownership of ministry outreach, and the position of youth worker is gaining greater respect. In the field of adolescent development, the church youth worker is now viewed as important as school teachers, principals, counselors, etc. As we enter into this new millennium, it will be truly historic if we join together and work not only to strengthen the students we now have, but reach those who don't stand a chance if we don't unify.

> "Neither do men pour new wine into old wineskins. If they do, the skins will burst, the wine will run out and the wineskins will be ruined. No, they pour new wine into new wineskins, and both are preserved."
>
> *Matthew 9: 17, NIV*

CHAPTER 15

The Next Step
Church-Assisting Organizations

Soon after celebrating a half-century of ministry as a traditional para-church youth organization, KCYFC started to sense that the organization's operating mode could not sustain a thriving future. We needed change and we needed it quickly. We were in the middle of a leadership transition from Dr. Al Metsker, the original founder, to his son Ronnie Metsker.

Fortunately, Ronnie had the vision and courage to avoid falling into a "we must maintain" mode. Ronnie is cut out of the contemporary, professional leadership mold. Knowing it would take several people to fill the extraordinary shoes of both Dr. Al and Vidy Metsker, Ronnie assembled a team of leaders. We knew we would have to embrace revolutionary change. There wasn't enough time for evolutionary change.

I like the way Ken Blanchard defines revolution:

> *Revolution means turning, changing direction. The act of revolving. It means the change required is significant, obvious even to the casual observer. It is more comforting to talk about evolutionary change. Evolutionary change means that everything is planned, under control and reasonably predictable.* [1]

Human nature resists change. This is a major reason why people lose touch, churches drift into irrelevance, and organizations become obsolete. It's not just a ministry problem. In his book, *The Fifth Discipline*, Peter Senge writes,

> *Few corporations live even half as long as a person. In 1983 a Royal Dutch/Shell survey found that one third of the firms in the Fortune 500 in 1970 had vanished. Shell estimated that the average lifetime of the largest industrial enterprises is less than forty years, roughly half the lifetime of a human being. The chances are fifty-fifty that readers of this book will see their present firm disappear during their working careers.* [2]

If individual churches and parachurch organizations have longer life spans than for-profit organizations, it is more likely related to one of two things.

> · The ministry organization is in tune with the Spirit of God and the culture in which the organization is working, therefore they are constantly growing and changing, or
>
> · The members of the ministry organization are committed at any and all cost to perpetuate the ineffective organization as a tribute to its past.

Sadly, there are too many ministry organizations in the second category.

Mark Senter, of Trinity International University, believes that parachurch agencies that attempt to reach the entire student population with a single strategy will not grow. Each agency has carved out a niche for ministry and has settled within the comfort zone of the portion of the youth culture they have targeted. The time has come for revolution – a total restructuring of youth ministry. It's not enough to modify the current structure. It cannot possibly keep up with the changes in the world in which we live. Youth ministry has grown old and its leaders have become conservators of treasured memories. [3]

Change is difficult. Managing change effectively and productively is even more difficult: we've never been here before, so how can we ascertain if

what we're doing will work? It takes strong leadership, good communication skills, constant vision casting, systems thinking and clear direction to
change people's fixed ideas or paradigms. In *Paradigms, The Business of
Discovering the Future*, the authors remind us that in order to shape our
future, we must be ready and able to change our paradigms. [4]

Shifting Gears, Sharing Vision

The greatest paradigm shifts needed for the sake of the Kingdom must
come from both the church and the parachurch. Churches must partner
with each other and act corporately, more like the entrepreneurial parachurch has typically acted. Likewise, youth ministry parachurch organizations must become servants of the local church; they must become
Church Assisting Organizations.

Why? Because local churches provide the most effective capability to do
incarnational, holistic student ministry, including youth ministry that con-
siders the context of the student within his or her family. In addition,
Church Assisting Organizations can bring a focus and leadership to the
overall, citywide structure.

The principle is twofold: we need both real change and unity in the body
of Christ. We must pursue win-win partnerships between churches and
other ministry organizations. Every city needs a coalition of local churches unified by Church Assisting Organizations that fulfill the apostolic role
of providing ministry structure that enables "The Church of [Our City]"
to impact the entire community. Stephen Macchia, President of Vision
New England, declares,

> *When what we do as parachurch leaders is done independent of the local
> church then we are counter-productive for the Kingdom. I prefer the term
> church-based ministry and choose to align with ministries who see the cen-
> tral thrust of their service as building up and encouraging those who lead on
> the front lines of local church ministry.* [5]

The exciting thing is that this paradigm is being grasped all over the country and may emerge as one of the most effective dynamics for reaching a city for Christ since the first century church.

Bob Buford is the founder of FaithWorks, an organization that focuses on building strategic partnerships. He's succinct: "It is important to ensure partners have the same values, but different and complimentary capabilities." [6] The key component in the partnership between Church Assisting Organizations and local churches is *shared values*.

Steps to Building a 21st Century Organization

As a large, highly visible, traditional parachurch organization beginning its second half-century of existence, KCYFC recognized it needed a radical, revolutionary change. We didn't want our mission to be the survival of an old wineskin. We started by making a major commitment to the research and study of change itself. We looked at the elements needed for successful dynamic change. The book *21st Century Organization* lists five components of radical change within an organization. [7]

- A bold vision

- A systematic approach

- A clear intent and mandate

- A specific methodology

- Effective visible leadership

A Bold Vision

In the process of KCYFC's transition we held several off-site planning sessions with our staff to do vision work. We took 100 full-time staff people on a three day retreat called "Scheme and Dream." Our entire focus was to dream big, think out of the box, ask "what if" questions like, "What would we do if human and financial resources were unlimited?" We challenged our staff to dream dreams so big they would almost be embarrassed to share their dreams of ministry results.

Other times we limited our journey to the Leadership Team. We talked about creating a new direction for the future. We brought in visionary leaders to challenge us. We heard people like Tom Peters, Zig Zigler, Bob Buford, and Tom Blanchard. We read and studied books. We debated intensely. We spent months working on Mission, Vision and Value statements for our new organization. Oftentimes, we involved our entire staff in the process. We prayed and sought the face of God.

Robert Rubin has said, "One way to judge if you are reengineering: the first time you bring something new up, if no one screams, 'Are you crazy?' then it is not a reengineering project." [8]

Gradually, we created a flexible learning environment. People became more creative and innovative. Before long we were willing to risk the entire organization to pursue what we felt God was calling us to do. I can't count all the times when one or another staff member had a "Are you (we) crazy?" moment. But there were plenty.

A Systematic Approach

We no longer wanted to be a traditional youth ministry parachurch organization. Our desire shifted to recreate ourselves as a Church Assisting Organization. We felt our Mission, "to bring youth into a growing relationship with Jesus Christ" would be more effective if we changed our paradigm. Through servant leadership, we wanted to facilitate a partnership – churches united with youth pastors, mobilized to take the Gospel to every secondary school student in a 100-mile radius around Kansas City.

We knew we would have to change many of the things we had been doing for years. We knew we would have to begin doing things we had never done before. We became organizational architects designing an infrastructure that would help us fulfill our new mission and vision.

· We evaluated successful programs, some of which we had enjoyed for decades.

- We shut down those programs that might conflict (or could even be perceived to conflict) with the local church.

- We committed ourselves to building relationships with pastors and youth pastors.

- We re-allocated job descriptions to allow more assistance in church ministry.

At this stage we were not broadcasting our actions or our future direction to those outside the organization. We just tried to model new behavior. We challenged each other with the importance of servant leadership.

A Clear Intent and Mandate

Churches and youth pastors began to take notice and comment about changes they were observing in our organization. The feedback was extremely positive. It was at this time that KCYFC became aggressive about verbalizing our Mission and Vision (to be a Church Assisting Organization). We also began to facilitate the creation of a Strategic Local Church Partnership.

- We surveyed youth pastors.

- We held focus groups to solicit input.

- We wanted to know what we were doing that was helpful and what we were doing that was not.

As a result of our findings, we made additional program changes.

The introduction to one of our initial youth pastor surveys stated:
KCYFC is experiencing a paradigm shift in regard to the way it approaches youth ministry. KCYFC is making efforts to unite local church youth workers to more effectively reach students in this city. Dr. Al and Vidy Metsker founded Kansas City Youth for Christ in 1943 at the same time as other youth movements were being formed in cities across the country. They realized that very little was being done to

reach high school students with the Good News of Jesus Christ. At that time, churches were not aggressively ministering to reach students, and youth pastors were nonexistent.

Times have changed. Churches are aggressively ministering to students and there are several hundred local church youth workers in the greater Kansas City area. KCYFC knows that to remain on the cutting edge, changes are necessary. KCYFC believes it can best fit into God's plan for reaching the youth in Kansas City by networking and servicing local church youth pastors.

Our mission is to bring youth into a growing relationship with Jesus Christ. We are concerned about what is getting done to get the Gospel to every student on every campus in the greater Kansas City area. Local church networks are the core for effective ministry on a broad scale. We believe Kansas City can demonstrate how local church youth pastors from different denominations can come together "in one spirit, with one mind and strive together for the faith of the Gospel" (Philippians 1:27). A God-given Mission and Vision will unite youth pastors and create an unstoppable force for the Kingdom of God. The following questionnaire is designed to help us better understand your heart and views.

A New Name

To put an exclamation point on our desire to change, we began an organizational transition from the name Kansas City Youth for Christ to the name *YouthFront.* This was one more way to reinforce our commitment to becoming a new organization.

In time, we became aggressive about casting our vision of forming a Strategic Local Church Partnership called the YouthFront Alliance. This alliance has quickly grown to over 200 youth pastors and over 300 churches representing 30 denominations.

A Specific Methodology

At this point we started treating the local church and its youth pastor as primary customers. Soon afterward a Kansas City senior pastor would term our conduct toward local churches and youth pastors as "wholesale customer" treatment. (The students of course being the "retail customers.") We stressed servant leadership to our staff. We brought in experts to do customer training and applied it to relationship building with the YouthFront Alliance youth pastors. Our staff became genuinely enthused to bend over backward to serve youth pastors. Too often this type of behavior is done to manipulate. However, when servant leadership is authentic, it is powerful. People gain influence as a natural by-product of real service.

We took a risk and hired eight additional full-time staff as YouthFront Area Coordinators to focus entirely on building relationships and servicing the YouthFront Alliance networks. These people are all youth ministry professionals who had reached the stage of youth ministry where they desired to mentor youth leaders.

In order to give youth pastors a greater say in our new Church Assisting Organization and to guide the development of our Strategic Local Church Partnership, the YouthFront Alliance, we had each of the 20 YouthFront Alliance networks select a representative to serve on a citywide Advisory Team. We meet on a regular basis and get feedback, make plans, pray and even play together. One of the coolest things is the general feeling not only among the Advisory Team but also throughout the YouthFront Alliance networks that we are all on the same team. Of course, we feel this way because we ARE all a part of the same team, *The Church, The Church in Kansas City!* We are working together in orchestration to pursue the vision of presenting the Good News of Jesus to 175,000 students in the greater Kansas City area. It is awesome.

As the Advisory Team has gained ownership of the citywide strategy, their feedback and input has become increasingly valuable. Authentic, mutual trust has developed. We have laid our hearts open to our Allies. We have guarded the trust relationship like the golden goose that it is. And from this relationship, open communication from youth pastors has been fostered. Interestingly, one of the issues that youth pastors chose to address within this new atmosphere is that we at YouthFront are too oversensitive about the protection of their interests.

The response from youth pastors to our change has been overwhelming. An example of this is a statement Scott Peterson made in an Advisory Team meeting. Scott is a youth pastor from College Church of the Nazarene, one of the area's mega-churches. "I came from a large city with a lot of parachurch organizations that tried to say and do some of the things you guys are doing. You are different, and have our interests at heart." Another example was when visionary youth pastor Craig Howard, of Olathe Bible Church, said to us in the presence of 18 other youth pastors, "I trust you guys."

Relying on open communication to provide flexibility in resolving issues is key to building a trustworthy partnership. [9] We told the Advisory Team, and subsequently all the YouthFront Allies, that we were changing a 56-year tradition of mailing promotional materials for our programs directly to students. Instead, we would send the promotional materials directly to youth pastors for distribution to their students. These youth pastors would decide what they wanted to promote. Many people expressed their disbelief. But we did it; we quit marketing directly to the students and started wholesaling, in a sense, to youth pastors.

This was another one of those paradigm shifts that we discussed as a staff where, at first, we heard many "Are you crazy?" comments. But guess what?! As a result of the YouthFront Alliance partnership – and primarily through the power of relationships with youth pastors – the results when we ceased promoting to students has defied conventional marketing logic. Today, more students than ever are involved, and they are involved together with their youth pastors. YouthFront's Saturday night Impact program is busting attendance records. Our 1999 summer camp season enrolled its highest number of campers – more than 4600 students registered for weeklong sessions. God is blessing! We continue to work with the YouthFront Advisory Team of youth pastors to further develop the design of our citywide organizational structure.

Here are the basics to success:

- A clear sense of mission, vision and values are foundational to build a citywide Strategic Local Church Partnership.

- An infrastructure that is both an effective and efficient vehicle to accomplish your goals must be developed.

- Implement programs that meet strict criteria for alignment with your overall strategic plan.

"I will always take a *first rate implementation plan* and a good strategy over a second rate implementation plan and a first rate strategy. Why? Because we know how to adjust and learn as we go forward, but if we can't implement, what good is strategy?"[10]

Effective and Visible Leadership

Words of partnership can't be words of manipulation. Rhetoric doesn't work. If our behavior is incongruent with our words, trust is shattered and partnerships collapse. Everyone becomes more committed to the endeavor when they have ownership. "The more people you give credit to, the bigger your network grows... the more help you get as you take on larger tasks," states Tom Peters. [11]

There are several ways we work to achieve this. For example,

- We take every opportunity to give credit to the youth pastors involved in the YouthFront Alliance for the success of the partnership.

- We use our publications to spotlight individual youth pastors in the Alliance.

- We print the names of youth pastors who sit on the Advisory Team.

· We occasionally list local churches involved in the Alliance.

· We involve youth pastors in planning, scheduling and other important aspects of leading the ministry.

The bottom line is that the vision is huge and it takes a total team effort to get the job done. The victory comes when God anoints our efforts and we synergistically work to accomplish great and mighty things.

A Challenge to Passionate Leaders

God uses passionate leaders who humbly accept God's call on their life. Leaders who will "dream big dreams and be willing to pay the price to see those dreams come true." [12] Most probably, individual parachurch and church efforts will continue to grow. Brian O'Connell, Director of Strategic Partnership Development with Interdev states, "just as strategic alliances and partnerships redefined the business community, they have also changed the paradigm of Christian ministry. As the body of Christ seeks to make a greater impact, we realize we must reduce duplication. We must leverage our precious resources through ministry partnerships." [13]

A Personal Challenge to Parachurch Workers

If you are involved in a traditional parachurch youth ministry organiza-tion, count the cost, and consider becoming a Church Assisting Organization. Reorganize everything you are presently doing and facili-tate a citywide Strategic Local Church Partnership. For an inclusive, city-wide effort to be established, someone or some group must step forward and build a non-denominational infrastructure. Why not you?

A Personal Challenge to Youth Pastors

If you are a youth pastor in a city, become involved in a youth pastor's net-work. If there isn't one, start one. If you're already in one, start casting the vision for a Strategic Local Church Partnership. Pray that God will raise up a leader (or leaders) to step into an apostolic role to establish structure for a strategic partnership in your city.

I agree with my friend, Sue Vogt, senior consultant for Strategic Networking with the Christian Management Association. Sue believes the next century will see a host of new strategic relationships among churches and parachurch ministries. As believers become more focused on building the kingdom instead of protecting ministry turf, we will find a growing spirit of cooperation that will bring a true spiritual harvest as we work together in sharing the Gospel. [14]

I would add that, in the area of youth ministry, parachurch youth organizations will have to radically change in order to spark widespread local church involvement in partnerships. I believe I can say this since I have been in parachurch youth ministry longer than I have been a church youth pastor.

I'll say it again. We parachurch youth guys, whose ministry organizations most likely started when churches weren't specializing in youth ministry, need to reevaluate what we're doing and how we're doing it. The church is awake and better equipped to bring youth into a growing relationship with Jesus Christ. We must all work together to build new exciting models for effective youth ministry in a new millennium. Let's dream bigger that we've ever dreamed before and pioneer the next wave of youth ministry innovation.

> **"One cannot manage change.
> One can only be ahead of it."**
>
> *Peter Drucker*

CHAPTER 16

Overcoming Obstacles
What Can Keep You From Reaching Your City?

I love to be part of youth worker groups and engage in intense dialogue and debate over youth ministry principles, philosophy and practical methodology. I have been in many, many forums where we discussed the future prospect of strategic partnerships, Church Assisting Organizations, citywide models, and a unified Church working in orchestration to reach youth. Invariably this leads to lengthy discussions on the obstacles to this emerging movement.

I've compiled two lists of obstacles taken from discussions with para-church and church youth workers. The first is a list of obstacles that hinder existing parachurch youth ministries from redesigning themselves as Church Assisting Organizations. This list contains the many roadblocks that KCYFC wrestled with (and now as YouthFront we are still wrestling with) during our transition. The second list illustrates issues that affect churches and youth pastors and create obstacles to embracing strategic, citywide, outward focused partnerships. Keep in mind that these are defi- nitely not exhaustive or all-inclusive lists.

Obstacles that Hinder Parachurch Organizations from Becoming Church Assisting Organizations

- Basing success on the number of students who come to our program events.

- Not letting go of old ways, old behaviors.

- Being timid about taking risks.

- Basing success on what we are doing rather than on what is getting done.

- Helping donors catch the new vision.

- Having difficulty in killing "sacred cows."

- Being *my kingdom* minded instead of *God's Kingdom* minded.

- Being territorial.

- Having a scarcity mentality vs. abundance mentality.

- Lacking obedience to the Word of God.

- The chaos of change is painful and disruptive.

- The culture of the old organization.

- Why stop doing something you have been doing successfully for decades?

Obstacles that Hinder Churches and Youth Pastors from Involvement in Outward-Focused, Citywide Partnerships

- Having an ownership instead of a stewardship orientation.

- Thinking we do not need to partner to succeed.

- Resistance from church leadership.

- Having a scarcity mentality vs. abundance mentality.

- Limitations on youth pastors' job descriptions.

- Lack of time.

- The attitude that our ministry is within the four walls of our church.

- Lack of Mission and Vision.

- Lack of trust.

- Having a predominant denominational focus.

We have already looked at one of the great challenges of leadership: how to effectively manage change. Real change means "challenging and discarding historical precedents, tried-and-true processes, and conventional wisdom and replacing them with entirely different concepts and practices. Traditional workflows must be examined and redesigned. New systems must be created. Ways of measuring success must be rethought." [2] Just reading these statements can seem exhausting. (How many times did you need to look them over? More than once? You're not alone!)

How can we stay ahead of change? Peter Drucker believes organizations need "change leaders" who focus on change as opportunity. Too often, instead of engaging in fundamental change, we settle for a no-risk superficial cosmetic makeover. Once again, Ken Blanchard: "Present pressures always seem to win out over future considerations. Thus, most organizational transformation agendas are more about improving the present than they are about creating the future." [3]

There are two ways for leaders to go about change:
> · Wait until the organization hits the wall, in which case they
> have no choice.

That's reactive change.

> · Scan the horizon for opportunity and plot a course to take
> advantage of it.

This is proactive change. [4]

A couple of times, at key intersections in the transition from a parachurch organization to a Church Assisting Organization, I remember telling our president, "I believe in this particular issue of change so strongly that I'm willing to put my job on the line. Fire me if it doesn't work." Of course, I must admit I stated my offer for effect, because I knew Ronnie was as willing to make changes as I was. In fact, KCYFC's leadership believed in the importance of change to the point where we were all willing to lay it on the line. I've asked staff members several times if they were willing to risk it all for the creative ideas they had. Fortunately, we have a team of innovative pioneers.

I remember a particular crucial moment in our transition. Mike Yaconelli, of Youth Specialties, was in Kansas City and five of our Leadership Team members were having dinner with him. As we shared our heart and vision with Mike, he stopped us and, with quivering lips, passionately stated that the Holy Spirit was laying a "God-thing" on us and that he sensed we were on "holy ground." Here we were, six grown men sitting in a crowded restaurant, speechless, tears rolling down our cheeks, trembling with emotion. God used significant moments like that to strengthen our resolve to continue the hard work of change.

It is so difficult to let go of the past and take a leap into the future. Dee Hock, a visionary business leader and creator of VISA states: "The problem is never how to get new, innovative thoughts into your mind, but how to get old ones out." [5]

Nothing stops an organization faster than people who believe that the way they worked yesterday is the best way to work tomorrow. Not only do we have to change how we act, but we must also change the way we think about the past. [6]

Joe Madonna, Chairman, KPMG International

Our tendency may be to eliminate all risks before we take that visionary leap into a new paradigm. But if we wait until all risk is thoroughly removed, we will never rise above mediocrity. We can't possibly have all the answers before we make a move. This is a journey, and half the success is in the commitment to get started.

Let's take a closer look at some of the biggest obstacles you may encounter on your journey. These issues can sidetrack your youth ministry efforts to engage in strategic partnership. If you are a youth pastor, these obstacles will fight against your desire to be outward focused in your church's ministry. If you're a parachurch youth worker, these issues will work as resistance to your desire to transition from a traditional parachurch model to a Church Assisting model.

Obstacles That Block Change

Lack of Focus

Research among senior pastors of Protestant churches revealed the following:

Less than one of every ten senior pastors can articulate what he believes is God's vision for the church he is leading. [7]

George Barna

This is important: start with a Mission and Vision focus. *Mission* deals with why your organization exists. *Vision* deals with your desired destination. How can you be focused if you don't know where you want to go or why you want to go there? Once you determine your desired destination you can deal with developing a vehicle (or strategies and programs) to get you to your desired destination. When you have clear direction it is easier to stay focused, to stay on course. And clear direction minimizes the temptation to take detours that consume time and resources. When you are in ministry the demands on you can be overwhelming and it is easy to stray off course. Barna goes on to say:

> It is very easy for a movement or revolution to get sidetracked. More often than not, the loss of momentum is due to internal dynamics, not because of external resistance. People get distracted, begin to accept the status quo, or lose their sense of fighting a meaningful battle against a deplorable enemy. [8]

Great success comes to those who can stay focused on the main things. Be diligent about doing those things that have high leverage. Read books that will help you develop personal mastery. They not only charge you with ideas and teachings to grow, they also keep you in touch with your focus.

The Comfort of the Comfort Zone

Those who reside in their comfort zone have never changed the world.

Aren't you glad Abraham left his comfort zone? And Queen Esther? How about the Apostle Paul? And Luther? And Dr. Martin Luther King Jr.?

We need to walk by faith not by sight. One of my favorite lines in the song, *Everybody's Free to Wear Sunscreen*[9], goes, "try one thing everyday that scares you." I don't know if I agree with the everyday part but I do think that often you should do things that force you out of your comfort zone. Your faith will not experience significant growth if you live out your life in the comfort zone. When I first returned to high school campuses to do student ministry – after being out of high school for many years – it was not comfortable. It was downright scary. I broke out in a sweat. Two thousand students in a Christian environment is my comfort zone. Two thousand students in a public school was definitely not my comfort zone.

Maintaining the status quo with how you conduct your youth ministry may be your comfort zone. Challenging the "protectors of the heritage" to become new wineskins may cause you to break out in hives. When you step out of your comfort zone remember that the only way to succeed is to be led by the Holy Spirit.

Fear

_____

Fear is related to our departure from the comfort zone.
It is risky business being a pioneer.

_____

No one who has been there will deny it: it's dangerous to be a paradigm-changer. Joel Arthur Barker proclaims, "New paradigms put everyone who practices the old paradigm at great risk. The higher your position in the organization, the greater the risk to you and the organization. The better you are at your paradigm, the more you have invested in it, the more you have to lose by changing paradigms." [10]

Fear of change will be one of your biggest obstacles to overcome. In order to stay in the comfort zone, people will come up with all kinds of reasons to resist change. History is full of examples of skeptics who did not see paradigm shifts on the horizon. Here are a few enlightening examples:

· A 1910 edition of *Scientific American* proclaimed that to affirm that the airplane is going to "revolutionize" naval warfare of the future is to be guilty of the wildest exaggeration.

· On November 16, 1929, The Harvard Economic Society agreed that a severe depression like that of 1920-1921 is outside the range of possibility.

· After concluding the non-aggression pact with Hitler in 1939, Stalin was so convinced the Germans would not attack that he ignored 84 warnings to the contrary.

· In 1943 Thomas J. Watson, then chairman of IBM, was quoted as saying that he believed there to be "a world market for about five computers."

· In 1977 Ken Olson, then president of DEC, stated that "there is no reason for any individual to have a computer in their home."

· In 1991, a senior executive from CBS told a congressional committee that digital television, "defies the laws of physics." [11]

No one likes to be scrutinized and criticized, but if you are doing bold things for God you will be criticized. Don't seek it, but expect it. Dream big and attempt great things for God. Don't be discouraged by those who don't believe in you.

Pride

We all know the folly of pride. Here are a few of the countless statements someone in your organization, including yourself, may utter along the way.

· "We don't need to partner with other churches. Our goal is to be a mega-church and we can reach the city by ourselves."

· "We don't need to become a Church Assisting Organization, instead the church can assist us – we are the specialists."

· "No one can do it better than we can."

There are far too many personal kingdom builders in ministry today. How we must grieve God when we fail to set aside our personal, existentially developed, idiosyncratic, puny plans in order to join hands with the Body of Christ and be the Church triumphant.

Control

Churches of the 21st century will not be those that emphasize self-preservation and isolation without risk. The survivors and thrivers will be those who exist for others. [12]

In genuine leadership it is a real art to find the harmony between *making things* happen and developing a creative environment that *encourages things* to happen.

Trying to control people and environments in an unhealthy way quickly leads to dysfunction. Some youth pastors are driven to protect their students and keep their group intact and under control. They don't want their students involved in anything except their official church or denominational events.

> In the traditional authoritarian organization, the dogma was managing, organizing, and controlling. In the learning organization, the new 'dogma' will be vision and values. [13]
>
> Peter Senge

I've seen some youth pastors who are so controlling that they would rather see their students be involved in a non-Christian event than another non-sanctioned, Christian ministry event. This mentality tends to have just the opposite effect that is desired. Committed Christian students with a solid biblical world-view want to connect with other like-minded students. They want to come together on campus, they want to hang together. The harder we try to control our students in an unhealthy manner, the more likely we are to either drive away our sharp students or develop students with non-biblical attitudes who will not be challenged to be salt and light.

We should not try to control our students. Let's empower them and equip them to come together with other students from other local churches and denominations to reach their friends for Jesus. This is the biblical model for growing our churches. Controlling students is not the answer!

Lack of Trust

> Do you mistrust others, thinking they'll somehow use your suggestions against you or take credit for your ideas? By holding back on trust, you stifle your own creativity and ultimately limit the growth of your [church, organization]. [14]

I believe we have long-grieved the Holy Spirit with our attitudes that our denomination, our church, our organization is right... the best... God's favorite. It is one thing to have disagreement on the historic fundamentals of the faith like the virgin birth, the deity of Christ, etc. These disagreements <u>should</u> lead to non-cooperation. But usually, the reason we don't work together has nothing to do with major doctrinal issues. Too often, our excuses for not joining forces are petty.

For the sake of reaching the lost world we live in, we need to have grace with each other. We must humbly acknowledge that we have minor, differing doctrinal views that will be taught within our individual churches. These doctrinal issues are important, but we must not allow our individual doctrinal views to conflict with God's desire for believers to be in unity as we work to reach the world.

In order to develop strong youth ministry partnerships to reach our cities we must create good communication systems. We must talk through the issues that concern us. I feel it is vitally important to define partnerships with a set of values that will serve as a code of conduct and create an environment where youth pastors can work together as the Church of [Our City].

Inflexible Culture

"Culture" refers to the norms of an organization, "the way we do things around here." It is reflected in people's behavior and language. An organization's culture is deep and complex, and based on the shared assumptions and beliefs of its members.[15]

In order to shift our youth group to an outward-focused youth ministry or to change the focus of our parachurch youth ministry from duplicating local church efforts, we have to deal with the existing cultures that embrace our old paradigms. We need new wineskins for the new wine.

The first step is to clearly articulate the vision and challenge the culture to do a paradigm shift. Let those who embrace the old culture have time to process: don't push so hard at first that you create more resist-ance. Ken Blanchard believes style of leadership is the primary driver in creating culture. It is a function of how decisions are made, communication flows, information is shared, motivation is generated, and conflict is handled. [16]

Spend time casting the vision to key people who will be able to use their influence with others. Let those who are comfortable with the old culture give feedback. Present logical, biblical, strategic reasons for change.

Then, and only then **proceed to do everything you can to challenge the existing culture in this group to accept change.** The more influence you have in the culture, the more leverage you will have as a *change agent.*

If you are a youth pastor, the key to substantial change will be the amount of alignment you have with the senior pastor and other church leadership. It will be a great enough challenge to change an inward-focused church culture with the pastor and other key leadership aligned with you. If they do not share the passion you have to reach non-churched students through on-campus ministry and a citywide partnership, you may find yourself in a no-win scenario. You may be faced with a situation where you have to decide if you will stay in your present position or move into a church environment that is compatible with your ministry philosophy and vision.

If you move into a new church:
Ask the church leadership as many questions as they ask you.

· Find out about their philosophy of ministry.

· Ask for the mission, vision and values of the church.

· Share your outward focus of empowering and equipping students for ministry.

· Ask about networking and partnering with other churches and denominations.

· Make sure the job description is compatible with incarnational student ministry.

- Do they want you in your office all the time – or do they get excited about you being out in the world of students?

- How will they measure your performance?

- Do they want a personality to build the youth group around – or do they want a leader who will train and empower others to help lead?

If you are a parachurch youth worker:
Approach the leadership of your ministry just as a youth pastor approaches the leadership of their church.

If you are a leader in a parachurch youth organization:
Approach the Board of Directors, major donors, and your staff. The key to motivating those around you toward change will be your passion and your ability to inspire others with your Vision: to become a Church Assisting Organization that will facilitate a Strategic Local Church Partnership to reach students more effectively.

When to Let Go
At one point in the early stages of KCYFC's transition, as is the case in most organizations that are undergoing change, there was a pocket of resistance. After numerous efforts to bring the resistance into alignment, our Leadership Team became very frustrated. Ronnie finally exclaimed, "If we can't change the inflexible culture, we will kill the culture." Several individuals were let go and suddenly the culture became much more pliable. This was not a strong-armed power move; it was an example of leadership doing the right thing at the right time in the right way. It was also appropriate for these individuals to leave; they had repeatedly demonstrated they were not going to be content in this new culture.

> It's generally much easier to kill an organization than to change it substantially. Organisms by design are not made to adapt... beyond a certain point. Beyond that point, it's much easier to kill them off and start a new one than it is to change them. [17]
>
> Kevin Kelly, author of "Out of Control"

This is not as hard-hearted as it sounds at first. Simply look at the history of science. It is an unbroken sequence of breakthrough discoveries. And new discoveries – from Galileo to the Wright brothers – are almost without exception, automatically dismissed by their culture. Major newspapers ignored the historic Wright brothers' flight of 1903 mainly because *Scientific American* claimed it was a hoax. Even worse, during the following five years they *continued* arguing that it was scientifically impossible! [18] Don't laugh – some youth ministry workers have been known to do the same type of thing.

Effective leaders need to spend a lot of time and energy investing in the creation of a flexible, learning environment and a healthy culture. Let's look more closely at Ken Blanchard's definition of culture introduced at the beginning of this section:

> *Culture is the norms of an organization, the way we do things around here. Culture is reflected in people's behavior and language. An organization's culture is deep and complex, and based on shared assumptions and beliefs of its members. Style of leadership is the primary driver in creating culture. It is a function of how decisions are made, communication flows, information is shared, motivation is generated, and conflict is handled.* [19]

Don't let this obstacle stand too tall.

The Wrong Definition of Success

> *How does our church or organization measure success?*
> *Is our goal to do a little bit better than last year?*

Even if norms and expectations are not clearly written, they exist. And they are always at work in our churches and parachurches. So, what are they? Take a look at the following list of questions...

> · Are we expected to fix those students who are challenging or wandering from the values of their parents who attend our church?

· Is the church satisfied if we keep the kids entertained?

· Are we expected to grow? If so, how?

· How do we want to see numerical growth?

· If a church youth group grows in numbers by hosting an exciting plethora of adventurous activities that Christian students in the community can't resist, is that success?

—————— OR ——————

· **How about measing success based on the number of Christian students who have accepted the challenge to be an on-campus missionary?**

· **What about measuring success based on the pursuit of our students to become committed growing disciples of Jesus Christ?**

Reggie McNeal states that outward focused congregations...

Not only risk involvement with the world, they strategize for it. Convinced that the harvest is ripe, these congregations search for ways to reach beyond the citadel and fortress of church real estate and programming. They measure their effectiveness through the number of transformed lives that enter into their community of faith from non-churched or under-churched backgrounds. [20]

How can we fulfill God's purposes for His Church in the world if we are not outward focused? In an interview in the *Win Arn Growth Report,* Dr. George Hunter, Dean of the School of World Mission at Asbury Seminary, described the kind of church that reaches persons outside the church. [21]

Churches that are effectively reaching secular people...

· know that people who aren't disciples are lost

· know that lost people matter to God

- see their church as primarily a mission to lost people rather than a gathered colony of the faithful

- have high expectations of their members

- know what to change and what to preserve

- understand secular people

- accept unchurched people

- use music secular people understand

- start new congregations

- are involved in world mission

What is our definition of success?

This is an extremely important question. If ever there was a need to know "What Would Jesus Do? (Say?)," it could be this critically important question related to our ministry efforts.

Job Descriptions

Job descriptions need to be compatible with the mission and vision of the organization and with the organizations' measures of success.

It is important to revisit this issue because all too often our job descriptions are based on the wrong definitions of success. It is one of *the* major frustrations for youth pastors.

Many feel their job description is written to emphasize that their ministry is to be conducted within the four walls of the church, period. One youth pastor was telling me how a church administrator caught him in his office one day. The administrator stressed how happy he was to have him there. Thinking he was appreciated for being on the church staff, the youth pastor responded, "I'm glad I'm here also." The church administrator clarified his statement by saying, "No, I mean I'm literally glad to see you here in your office working."

The implication was, of course, "I don't see you around here much so you must not be working." The youth pastor responded by asking, "What does the title on my office say?" The church administrator replied, "Youth Pastor." To this the youth pastor asked, "Do you see any youth in here?" The point, hopefully, was well taken.

Youth ministry is about being with youth. This is how Jesus did His ministry: He was with people. Many youth pastors are so busy planning and preparing programs and events they don't have time to be with students.

One of our desires as a Church Assisting Organization is to develop and administer programs that youth pastors can utilize for their church programs. We'll do the behind the scenes work so they can spend time being youth pastors to their students.

When KCYFC began the transition from parachurch to Church Assisting Organization, some of our youth workers on staff who had the desire to be with kids did not like our new focus on working more directly through youth pastors. Although we feel that our staff does need to be directly involved with students, our new role would require more involvement with youth pastors and service to churches. Some of our staff left to work in a more incarnational capacity through local churches and now benefit from the services we provide them.

Lack of Resources

*If Christians began to give in a biblical manner
there would be billions of new dollars available for reaching the world.*

"If I had more money and workers I could be a lot more successful youth worker." Certainly every youth worker has thought or even said this at one time or another. And it is probably a true statement, but it doesn't have to be a loser's limp to rationalize our mediocrity. When we become impassioned about the vision that God has placed on our hearts, resources will become available.

· Money

People want to be involved in something bold and noble. We know it is God's will that "ALL should come to repentance." We are aligned with God when we become consumed with encouraging, equipping and empowering Christian students to be the salt and light and win their friends to Jesus. We must give lay leaders the privilege of joining us in our youth ministry efforts to make disciples of students. When people get involved with their time, they will also get involved with their money. If Christians began to give in a biblical manner, there would be billions of new dollars available for reaching the world.

> *When it comes to giving, people in today's culture – including Christians – have moved from the biblical definition of money (ie: giving out of charity, love, and grace) to a human-centered definition of money (giving to get something back).* [22]

· People Power

In terms of human resources, we must enlarge our impact on the lives of students by enlisting other committed adults to become youth workers. We should not limit our search for adult lay youth leaders to parents or young adults. If an adult is walking with God and has a passion for student ministry, plug them in somewhere. Some of the best youth workers I know defy the picture of an ideal youth worker.

> *Wendell is 78 years old. He is African-American, and most of the students he has contact with at church are white. Wendell always has an encouraging word to say to students. He challenges them to walk with God. He's still a growing person and completed Bible college last year. Wendell is a blessing to students and they know he loves them.*

Dave became a youth worker at age 42. He got involved because he wanted to see his own teenage children find Christ. They did, and 25 years later at the age of 67 he is still actively involved in youth ministry. When a student that he has developed a relationship with misses church he calls them. He goes to sporting events and school events. Students call him Grandpa. In fact, he couldn't wait until he retired so he could devote all his time to youth ministry. Dave King, my father, is a better youth worker than I will ever be. On Saturday nights, Dave gets on a church bus with my mother, Wanda, and takes a load of screaming middle school students to Impact. He cooks hamburgers for high school students at a coffeehouse. The loud music isn't his style but it doesn't bother him; it's just another chance to be with kids. I believe he will do youth ministry until the day he dies.

Our churches are filled with Wendells and Daves, along with parents who care, and others who are waiting for us to challenge them to get involved in life-changing ministry with students. Their help can enable us to spend more time on campus, more time with students, and more time working with other youth pastors and churches in a strategic partnership of city reaching.

Isolationism

A youth ministry that is inwardly focused leads to isolation.

There is a lot of confusion about what it means to be in the culture/world but not of the culture/world. The mindset that "I must isolate my teenagers from the culture/world to protect them from evil" leads to dysfunctional Christianity. Christ is not against culture. Christ is against sin. Christ *engaged* culture. He commands us to be salt and light within culture. This is not always easy to do.

As parents we want to protect our kids. Our challenge is to train them how to stand strong in the midst of a culture that is often adversarial to the things of God. We need to train them how to think critically and biblically guide them through the experiences they encounter in their culture/world.

A parent of one of the students in my youth group was not happy about our outward focused ministry strategy. In the course of outlining his dissatisfaction, he stated, "I work hard to pay for my son to attend Christian school so that he won't be influenced by non-Christian friends, only to have you stress that our kids need to have non-Christian friends. Non-Christians are attending your activities and programs and those kids are a bad influence on my son."

I know you probably don't believe that this was an actual quote. But I can still hear those words bouncing around in my head. The comments were made during a church youth ministry parents' meeting. Fortunately, it was so absurd I didn't even have to respond directly. I could tell that other parents were as shocked as I was. Usually, most of the people who believe in maintaining a comfortable isolation from the culture/world, won't make such blatantly anti-biblical statements. However, I've found they like to interject their subtle philosophy of isolationism most every chance they have.

Some form of this isolation mentality is what motivates certain parents to send their teenagers to Christian school. There may be some good reasons for parents to choose a Christian school for their teenage student. However, I think the best plan is for parents to mentor their children to represent the Kingdom of God as salt and light in the real world.

> *This kingdom mind-set change is also something of a shift in theology, with a growing emphasis on 'the priesthood of the believer.' Some characterize it as a second Reformation in which God's work is being returned to the people; the pastor is seen less as the primary kingdom worker and more as the facilitator of kingdom work, which is done through God's people.*

> *Church pastors with kingdom eyes are not looking for more church workers, but instead are challenging their people to be agents for Christ, deployed to their world, rather than huddled in the sanctuary of the church.* [23]

Scarcity Mentality

In youth ministry, abundance comes through the careful development of strategic, outward-focused, ministry mission and vision.

Some people – yes, even people in youth ministry – have the mindset that "I must hoard what is mine and protect it at all cost." This mentality is the antithesis of biblical principles like "give and it shall be given unto you," and "to gain life you must give your life away." With God as our source, there are enough students for every church to have as many students as they can accommodate. There are enough resources to go around because our heavenly Father is wealthy. We should have an abundance mentality.

Again, Dr. Leith Anderson,

> There is a sense in which the church has taken itself too seriously. We have thought that keeping ourselves going is a good enough reason to continue. How different from Jesus, who came to seek and to save those who were lost (Luke 19:10). The church is really a means to an end rather than an end itself. God is the one who is most important. Obeying Jesus Christ is what really matters. Keeping an organization going that meets in a building on the corner of Third Avenue and Main Street isn't really that important. Think about it: How many local churches have lasted anyway? Start with the church in Jerusalem, and make a list that includes the churches in Antioch, Ephesus, Corinth, and a million others – most of them are long gone. What matters is that THE church of Jesus Christ is larger and stronger than ever, that the gospel has more adherents right now than in all previous history combined, and that the cause and kingdom of the Savior have advanced for 2,000 years. [24]

The Church is at a Crossroads

George Barna believes that The Church is at a crossroads.

> It must decide if it wishes to defend its traditional structure, as represented by the congregational format, for the delivery of ministry benefits and opportunities, or if it will reengineer itself in a way that allows it to conform to its

biblical mandate and still respond to the practical needs of its members. This is an incredibly significant decision. [25]

He goes on to say,

> *Another strategy for congregational churches to pursue is to enter into strategic partnerships or alliances with other ministries – including parachurch ministries. For many years there has been an uneasy existence between the local church and parachurch organizations. Local churches have been wary of parachurch groups taking the time, money, energy, and attention of church members. Parachurch agencies have sometimes shown little respect for the ministry efforts of churches, especially when those efforts were in the building stage.*
>
> *The average Christian doesn't care about which organization gets credit, or institutional loyalty. People have very limited resources and are focused on the bottom line rather than on peripheral matters. It is time to eliminate territorial battles between churches and parachurch groups and to focus on kingdom outcomes. In the coming years congregational churches may find that they can achieve their vision more effectively by pruning their own roster of programs, downsizing staff, and working in tandem with parachurch ministries that specialize in specific ministry endeavors.*
>
> *There are many advantages to this process, among them the reduction of congregational overhead and liabilities, the expansion of the community of saints beyond the walls of the congregation, and the decentralization of the congregational entity (without jeopardizing the focus).* [26]

It's Time to Decide

We have discussed many dynamic forces at work that have created within youth ministry an environment for the emergence of citywide Strategic Local Church Partnerships and Church Assisting Organizations. Perhaps the success of this model of a unified citywide church working together depends on how effectively we each engage in the spiritual warfare to overcome the obstacles we encounter.

· Do you believe God is anointing a spontaneous, emerging movement of strategic, citywide youth ministry partnerships?

· Are you ready to overcome the obstacles hindering your involvement in this exciting move by God?

· If this model exists in your city, are you involved?

· If this structure has not been implemented in your city, what part will you play in launching it?

My heart burns with the potential of what God could do through a unified Church. We must pray that God will allow us to be obedient to His Spirit and be pliable enough to accept new wine. Some people will not be willing to change. However, we cannot fixate on those believers who are not willing to work strategically together.

> *When the builders laid the foundation of the temple of the Lord, the priest in their vestments and with trumpets, and the Levites (the sons of Asaph) with cymbals, took their places to praise the Lord, as prescribed by David king of Israel. With praise and thanksgiving they sang to the Lord: "He is good; his love to Israel endures forever." And all the people gave a great shout of praise to the Lord, because the foundation of the house of the Lord was laid. But many of the older priests and Levites and family heads, who had seen the former temple, wept aloud when they saw the foundation of this temple being laid, while many others shouted for joy. No one could distinguish the sound of the shouts of joy from the sound of weeping, because the people made so much noise. And the sound was heard far away.*
>
> *Ezra 3:10-13*

It was a great day. God was at work in a dynamic new way. The foundation of a new temple was being laid. Most of the people had a profound sense of excitement and wonder for what God was doing and they were ready to receive His lead for a new direction in their lives. They were shouting for joy. However, some people – "many of the older priests and Levites and family heads, who had seen the former temple" (v. 12) were weeping because they didn't want to let go of the past.

Some pastors, youth pastors, church leaders, denominational leaders and parachurch leaders are going to weep instead of shout for joy over the issues discussed in this book because they are threatened by change. Most, though, will shout for joy that God is working and things are changing.

Which group will you be in?

SECTION 5

POST LEAP

> *The real act of discovery consists not in finding new lands but in seeing with new eyes.*[1]
>
> *Marcel Proust*

CHAPTER 17

What Could Happen?

We live in an age when the key concepts associated with success are innovation, new paradigms, strategic organizational alliances and partnerships, mission, vision and values. And yet, could it be possible that the best chance to embrace those concepts and apply them to the new wineskin of strategic, citywide youth ministry is to reproduce a 2000-year-old model of the first century church?

> *The first-century Church was distinguished by its attitude. Specifically, the Christians of the day felt a sense of urgency about ministry. Not knowing when Christ would return, acutely aware that the ministry agenda He had outlined was of the utmost significance, they felt the need to be diligent about ministry. They also exhibited an intense passion for Christ and serving Him with their lives. And they were committed to doing their service with excellence because they knew it reflected their own depth of commitment to Christ.* [2]

If we are to succeed in our effort to make a quality, relationship-based presentation of the Gospel to every secondary student in North America, we must make a commitment to pursue a citywide partnership with others who share our vision.

> *Cities are central to God's redemptive strategy. The Great Commission begins with a city – Jerusalem – and culminates when another city – the New Jerusalem – becomes God's eternal dwelling with His people. In order to fulfill the Great Commission, we must reach every city on earth with the Gospel.* [3]

This book has focused on strategic citywide partnerships of local church youth pastors who work together in unity to reach the youth of their cities. Evangelism, through Equal Access Campus Clubs, has provided the spark to initiate these partnerships. Those cities that have already developed these partnerships were quick to realize the powerful potential of this new movement: a united cross-denominational citywide effort to fulfill all of the New Testament purposes of a church.

The youth Church of [Our City] can come together, not only for evangelism, but also for worship, fellowship, discipleship, and service.

A new work environment is also emerging from this movement. Long before Microsoft became a household name, there were plenty of effective programs for word processing, spreadsheets, database management, scheduling, etc. Then Microsoft created a new computing system by developing Windows. Windows isn't just a program; it is a revolutionary software environment that these other programs can operate *within*. This new environment made all PC applications more user-friendly, regardless of whether or not they were Microsoft-created programs. This is happening with citywide Strategic Local Church Partnerships. A new work environment is being introduced in which existing programs can not only become more effective, but also actually thrive on a whole new level.

The YouthFront Alliance in Kansas City is relatively young, and yet the networks and the Youth Pastors Advisory Team are already dreaming beyond Equal Access. The power of the YouthFront Alliance is *not* the Club121 Equal Access program. The miraculous power of the YouthFront Alliance is the real and dynamic unity among hundreds of youth pastors and churches.

It is now apparent that the tremendous evangelistic results we experienced through the YouthFront Alliance efforts can also be duplicated to produce successful results along with other purposes of the church, such as worship and service. For example, plans are being implemented to engage students in service through a citywide missions model. We have witnessed what happens when Christian students from nearly 500 churches work together on campus with a clear and common strategy. This success makes it easier to imagine what could happen if all of our students worked together to serve through a common mission strategy.

The FLOOD™ Strategy

Through a series of YouthFront meetings, a new strategy called FLOOD™ is being launched. FLOOD™ is about working together to "FLOOD the World with the Good News of Jesus Christ." It is based on Acts 1:8, "But you will receive power when the Holy Spirit comes on you; and you will be my witnesses in Jerusalem, and in all Judea and Samaria, and to the ends of the earth."

The F in FLOOD™ stands for Friends. Youth pastors want to emphasize to their Christian students the importance of having a ministry to their friends. The non-Christian friends at school are the primary mission field, their Jerusalem. Multiple strategies and training efforts will go into equipping and empowering Christian students to be missionaries on their school campuses. The emphasis will be on relationship evangelism and the utilization of the Equal Access Club as a primary tool for introducing their friends to Jesus.

The L in FLOOD™ stands for Local – it involves mission and service projects to needy areas of our city. The goal is to have thousands of Christian students working together to make a difference in Kansas City through their service. This is all about caring for people's needs, helping our community be a better place, and lending a hand of compassion to people who may not see love demonstrated very often. Partnerships have been developed between YouthFront and various ministries and churches, primarily in the urban core.

Instead of isolated, disconnected youth group efforts, the dream is to have the sustained and consistent involvement of Christian students and their churches in the community. The Youth Church of Kansas City is working together as salt and light in the city.

The first O in FLOOD™ stands for Outlying areas. As students serve as missionaries in their schools and communities, opportunities will be developed to enable students to serve outside their school and city. We've known that each year dozens of youth groups from Kansas City go to Mexico for summer mission trips. What if we all went to the same place? What if we all adopted a city or village in Mexico? What if there was continuity in our efforts? This summer, youth groups from Kansas City will do mission work in Monterrey, Mexico. For ten straight weeks, youth groups will arrive on Saturday and stay until the following Sunday. Each week will feature a 24 hour overlap so that the ministry baton can be passed from one Kansas City youth group to another.

The second O in FLOOD™ stands for Overseas. At one point in our transition to a Church Assisting Organization, we announced to the youth pastors Advisory Team that we were leaning toward scaling back our successful overseas student missions efforts – we didn't want to create competition with local church mission trips. To our surprise, many told us that they didn't want us to stop our efforts in this area. Some youth pastors were successfully running their own overseas mission trips, but others wanted YouthFront to offer mission trips as a resource for leadership development for some of their students. One change we did make was to stop marketing mission trips to students directly. Now the youth pastor is the recruiter for their students' involvement in YouthFront Missions.

Youth pastors are now leading YouthFront overseas trips, and we're helping other youth pastors design their own trips. As the students go through leadership development and discipleship, the overseas mission trip will be a tool at the youth pastor's disposal. When a student goes on an overseas mission trip they will be challenged to return home and make an impact on their school through their campus club, Club121.

The D in FLOOD™ stands for Development. The entire mission plan is to develop student leaders with a Christian world view. Curriculum and training materials tie the whole plan together. Because the youth pastors are working together with Club121 and other YouthFront programs, it all begins to fit together in a comprehensive citywide strategy.

YouthFront International Training Conferences

Tony Campolo, noted sociologist, commented that,

> In most of the "Two-Thirds nations," youth work is almost completely ignored by missionary organizations. Ironically, we've ignored youth ministry as a form of foreign missions, even though 90 percent of the population in the Two-Thirds nations are under the age of 25, and more than 30 percent of the population are teenagers.[4]

The startling discovery that 97 percent of the world's professionally trained youth workers are in North America, and that they're working with only 3 percent of the world's teen population, challenged us to train more international youth workers. Youth workers from the YouthFront Alliance are using their experience and expertise to train youth workers in other countries.

YouthFront International Association has been launched with hundreds of International Associates. After receiving training through a YouthFront International Training Conference, the youth workers apply to be an International Associate. These Associates will be able to communicate to Kansas City youth workers via the Internet and will be able to obtain resources through the YouthFront website. There's an additional benefit to these training conferences: the expansive development of relationships among K.C. youth workers that occurs during the trips. Once again, the emphasis of these efforts is an outward instead of an inward focus.

The citywide Strategic Local Church Partnership among Kansas City area youth pastors has been very rewarding. Youth pastors talk about a new level of teamwork, relationships, and fulfillment that has come through connection with each other. Youth pastors are developing deep friendships with one another across denominational affiliations. They are praying together, dreaming together, playing together and working together.

The Welcome Packet

As a Church Assisting Organization we devote a great deal of time and resources on strengthening and deepening the YouthFront Alliance because we believe that a strong, unified structure will experience incredible results. When a new youth pastor comes to a Kansas City church, YouthFront greets them with a Welcome Packet containing:

· City map

· Coupons for youth group activities

· Certificates for area restaurants

· Resource ideas

Youth pastors in the YouthFront Alliance are becoming passionate recruiters for other youth pastors to be a part of what is happening. In August of each year we host a Leadership Summit to train students in how to lead Club121 on their campus. At the one this past year I noticed a youth pastor that I had never met and introduced myself to him. He informed me that he had just moved to Kansas City "a few days ago" to begin serving as youth pastor in a church here. He went on to tell me that another youth pastor had called him up and insisted, "you just have to be at the Summit." The YouthFront Alliance youth pastor who had called him knew there was a school in his area without a Club121 and was doing his best to recruit this new youth pastor. Talk about a quick connection – this new youth pastor hadn't even met the students in his church yet.

While this emerging citywide Strategic Local Church Partnership model is still in the embryonic stage, we feel it contains great potential for the future.

What Is Possible? And When?

What could happen? Where could this lead? What is possible? It is safe and biblical to say, "if God is in it, nothing is impossible."

Within weeks of Jesus' departure, the disciples were accused by the religious experts in Jerusalem of having fulfilled the Great Commission in that city. Speaking on behalf of the council of elders, the high priest told them, *"You (the disciples) have filled Jerusalem with (His) teaching" (Acts 5:28)*. How much time elapsed between Acts 1:8 and Acts 5:28? Just a few weeks! In a matter of weeks, the Church went from the Upper Room to every living room in Jerusalem. [5]

One of the most motivational verses in the Bible for me is Acts 19:10 which says,

All who lived in the province of Asia heard the word of the Lord.

The Apostle Paul strategically delivered the Gospel to every person in Asia Minor from his organizational base in Ephesus!

One of the most frequently stated hopes among youth pastors in Kansas City is, "We want our senior pastors to have what we have." Unlike other cities affected by this emerging movement, Kansas City does not have a strategic, citywide partnership network of senior pastors, or worship leaders, or Christian educators, etc.

The Minneapolis/St. Paul, Minnesota area has a more developed model in which a representative from each of the citywide networks of senior pastors, youth pastors, prayer leaders, worship leaders, etc. form an executive citywide church team. They are working together as the Church of the Twin Cities to impact their cities for Jesus in unique ways. Please review the *Twin Cities Case Study*, by Dan Buschow, (*See Appendix B*) for a closer look at what God is doing there.

Where Are We Going?

We have been commanded to fulfill a commission – the Great Commission. A unified church is an essential part of God's plan for this to be accomplished. We must commit to God's agenda, not ours. There is, undoubtedly, openness within the Church today to come together and engage in unified movements of God.

And When Will We Go?

A new apostolic reformation of unity is a common theme of discussion among those engaged in ministry today. All seem to be in agreement that the Church should embrace unity and eschew divisions. However, confusion about the practical application of what a unified church looks like and does is hindering the potential, powerful impact that a citywide, first century model could have.

> *When the Church walks in unity, expressing the fullness of Christ, the forces of evil are displaced from the heavenlies and confined under the feet of Jesus. Now the Church is in control of the battleground. According to Jesus, this unity is what causes the world to believe. It is no coincidence that the expression "and the Lord added to their number daily those who were being saved" (Acts 2:47) appears in the context of the highest level of unity ever achieved in the Church. In that context, the fullness of Christ was at its highest, and Satan's stronghold on the lost at its lowest.* [6]
>
> *Ed Silvosa*

The ultimate biblical purpose for a citywide, unified church is not window-dressing to show the size of the church. The source of power of a unified Church is not the largeness of organizational numbers. The purpose of unity is to be a demonstration of Truth. God is not anxiously waiting for us to get unified so that he has enough of an army to change a city. God is all-powerful. God instructed Gideon, in Judges 7, to reduce the Israelite Army from 32,000 soldiers to 300 soldiers as a prerequisite to defeating the huge Midianite Army. In Judges 7:2,

> *The LORD said to Gideon, "You have too many men for me to deliver Midian into their hands. In order that Israel may not boast against me that her own strength has saved her."*

Reaching a city is not about numbers!

It's Not About Us. It's About God.

> *To Jesus, ministry was about the development of people's character, not about building bigger and better organizations. His interest was in disseminating truth principles, not crafting organizational policies. He measured victory not by the number of seats filled in the synagogue, but by the number of hearts transformed in the marketplace.*[7]
>
> George Barna

It is the will of God that we come together in unity. A unity based not on a success criteria of organizational size but on a foundation of Truth. This is why a Doctrinal Statement (*Appendix A*) and a Set of Values (Chapter 12), that all in the partnership agree on, is so essential for a citywide church partnership to succeed.

The power of the Holy Spirit is what will bring about the supernatural results from the display of Truth by a unified Church of [Our City]. Our faith is not in our strategic, citywide partnerships or in those who organize those structures. Our trust must be in the Word of God and the power of the Holy Spirit to bring awakening and revival. I believe that through God's plan of a unified, citywide, strategic church partnership, supernatural victories can be experienced.

Youth workers seem to be blazing the trail for this emerging movement. Perhaps through the strength of a spirit-led citywide effort we can overcome some of the great challenges that have perplexed those in youth ministry.

Dealing With Overlooked Issues

Most of the professional youth ministry in North America is targeted to middle-class suburbia. If we are truly going to fulfill the Great Commission of systematically giving every person the opportunity to hear the Gospel, we must work diligently to reach many of the overlooked or forgotten student groups in our society.

The Urban Core: Reaching Minorities

How can we reach students in the urban core? The only thing that can turn around the seeming hopelessness in our city centers is the Good News of Jesus. Working together, in the power of the Holy Spirit, we can commit ourselves to make a difference in our cities.

The Census Bureau informs us that while Caucasians presently account for three out of four Americans, by 2050 only half of the nation will be Caucasian. For this reason, multiculturalism will be increasingly significant in our language, customs, values, relationships, and processes. [8]

In The Coming Revolution in Youth Ministry, and Its Radical Impact on the Church, Mark Senter states, "Urban/suburban linkages will be vital in breeding new strategies for youth ministry. Minority groups scattered across metropolitan areas will create networks of youth ministry transcending the boundaries of school districts and municipalities." [9]

We are encouraged in Kansas City as urban and suburban youth workers join together. In addition, their students have come together as brothers and sisters to do ministry. At the 1998-99 school year's Kick-off Rally for the citywide launch of Club121, youth pastors worked together to create a talent lineup that would be appealing both to suburban and urban students. Seven thousand students with a strong, ethnic diversity from both the city's core and the suburbs mixed together. Popular music groups God's Property and Jars of Clay were a hit with all. This was only a step, but intentional plans are being implemented to unite the Church from every part of the city.

Who's Falling through the Cracks?

The answer, in part, includes:

> · Neglected students

> · Non-churched youth

> · Non-evangelical church youth

How can we move beyond the exclusive target group of the all-American student (somewhere between 25-40 percent of the student population) that most youth ministries tend to focus on? How can we reach the neglected students?

Today's middle school and high school campuses are a diverse mix of people groups and must be targeted strategically if we are to reach them. Additionally, there are students who are not connected to a church. Even more challenging is the question, "How do we reach those students who are connected to a religious group that is not evangelical?" Some traditional parachurch youth organizations that have focused on these student groups have made a great impact because many non-evangelical parents find it easier to allow their teenager to attend parachurch type events than it is to let them attend an organized local church. Following up with these students after they have made a decision for Christ is a real challenge without the resource of an evangelical local church connection. Because many of these students cannot become connected to an evangelical church (in many cases this is because of family involvement in a non-evangelical religious group), how will they receive spiritual instruction and discipleship?

We are still wrestling with these issues in our transition from a traditional youth ministry parachurch model to a Church Assisting Organization. While I believe it is innovative to become a Church Assisting Organization and facilitate a Strategic Local Church Partnership, it is not innovative to focus only on those students who are connected to an evangelical local church – especially if our top priority is evangelism.

We don't have all the answers. We are engaged in ongoing dialogue with youth pastors to find the answers. At least part of the answer lies in the paradigm shift youth pastors are making toward an outward-focused ministry not confined to the four walls of their church. Another part of the answer may lie with youth pastors who recognize the value of a citywide Church Assisting Organization that can target student groups not reached by individual local churches.

These are just some of the issues that are being examined. The optimistic potential is that a citywide strategic network of youth pastors is wrestling with these issues. Many "what if?" scenarios are being discussed.

Preparing for the Future.

Organizations and communities that learn to work together, that know how to learn together, that trust one another, and that become more expansive and inclusive, develop the capacity to deal with the unknown. They create a capacity for working and thinking together that enables them to respond quickly and intelligently to whatever the future presents [10]

What could happen, if the churches in your city came together as the Church of [Our City]? God only knows, but I believe the results will be no less spectacular than what happened in the book of Acts.

> the Power of **Relationships**
> +
> the Power of **Unity**
> +
> the Power of **Partnerships**
> +
> the Power of **Shared Mission, Vision** and **Values**

> the Power of **Prayer**
> and
> the Power of the **Holy Spirit**

= Revival, Awakening, City Reaching and Supernatural Kingdom Building

Who Will Embrace a Shared Vision?

The movie "*Spartacus*" was about a gladiator-trained slave who led an army of fellow slaves against the Roman Legions in 73 BC. Spartacus' slave army of nearly 100,000 defeated the Roman Legions seven times, but was finally crushed by Marcus Licinius Crassus after a long siege and battle at Lucania. In the book *The Fifth Discipline*, Peter Senge examines the power of shared vision portrayed in a scene from this classic movie.

In the movie, Crassus tells the 1000 survivors in Spartacus' army, "You have been slaves. You will be slaves again. But you will be spared your rightful punishment of crucifixion by the mercy of the Roman Legions. All you need to do is turn over to me the slave Spartacus, because we do not know him by sight."

After a long pause, Spartacus (played by Kirk Douglas) stands up and says, "I am Spartacus." Then the man next to him stands up and says, "I am Spartacus." Then the man next to him stands up and says, "I am Spartacus." And again, another man stands and also says, "No, I am Spartacus." Within a minute, everyone in the army is on his feet declaring himself to be Spartacus.

It doesn't matter whether this story is apocryphal or not. It demonstrates a deep truth: each man, by standing up, chose death. But the loyalty of Spartacus' army was not to Spartacus the man. Their loyalty was to a *shared vision* which Spartacus had inspired – the idea that they could be free men. This vision was so compelling that no man could bear to give it up and return to slavery.

A shared vision is not an idea. It is not even an important idea such as freedom. It is, rather, a force in people's hearts, a force of impressive power. It may be inspired by an idea, but once it goes further – if it is compelling enough to acquire the support of more than one person – then it is no longer an abstraction. People begin to see it as if it exists. Few, if any, forces in human affairs are as powerful as shared vision. [11]

Now is the time to embrace the shared vision of this emerging movement of citywide, strategic partnership as the Church of [Our City]. Be a leader, share this vision, and cast it wide. Don't wait until later to jump on board.

It's always a small minority of people who are able to discern current challenges and future trends. In I Chronicles we read the story of a great army that came to Hebron to make David their king. Among the 340,000 fighting men of this army was a tiny group of men from Issachar, numbering 200 men plus their families. But there was something about these 200 men from Issachar that set them apart from the crowd. We find them described as "those who had understanding of the times, to know what Israel ought to do" (I Chronicles 12:32). [12]

We desperately need visionary men and women to provide innovative leadership for The Church in our cities. Barna exclaims,

> *New leaders must be entrepreneurs. Entrepreneurship is not just starting something from scratch. It is the ability to make something succeed. They see the opportunities in the changes and strategize to turn those opportunities into good for God's Kingdom and Christ's church.* [13]

Are you going to be there?

I go where the puck is going to be, not where it is. [14]
Wayne Gretzky

I agree with C. Peter Wagner, from Fuller Theological Seminary, that the primary target for God's spiritual armies must be the cities of the world. Not that other evangelistic targets are passe or unimportant. We must continue our aggressive efforts to evangelize groups of people and individuals in every nation, religion, and rural population – reaching unsaved souls wherever they may be found. But let's be clear: nothing is more important in our day than reaching our cities.[15] And, to accomplish this, we must be willing to set aside our personal agendas for the Kingdom's agenda. If we do, we will be amazed at the results.

For many of us in the midwest, it wouldn't be a true summer night without the pleasant sound of cicadas, commonly known as locusts, musically buzzing their rhythmic songs. The summer of 1998 was a unique summer for these insects. When a cicada egg hatches, the nymphs burrow into the ground for either 13 or 17 years, depending on the species.[16] What made the summer of 1998 so unique was that both the 13 and 17-year cicada cycles coincided, and a bumper crop of both species emerged from the soil. At times the rhythmic buzzing of the cicadas was so loud you could hardly carry on a normal conversation outside. And yet the music was mesmerizing and beautiful. Instead of singing solos, the cicadas joined in a harmonic undulation of sound. They were in orchestration. They were in unity.

A new apostolic reformation of unity leading to the emergence of strategic, citywide ministry partnerships, not only of youth workers but the entire church, sounds beautiful. It sounds biblical. It sounds like our cities could be transformed with the life-changing message of Jesus Christ. Imagine what a beautiful sound it will make when we all start singing together – a non-compromising harmony of truth, to our city. It can happen if we boldly go where God wants to take us.

Thank God there has been a paradigm shift of God's work, from church and parachurch-centered to Kingdom-centered.

God is moving us. We know He is pleased by our unity and that He is not willing for cities of people to perish. Seek God's face, find out where He is moving, and go there! Don't be a spectator. Be a part of something historic for the Kingdom of God. It is worth remembering something else Wayne Gretzky said: "You miss 100 percent of the shots you don't take." [17]

The Time is NOW!

It's the beginning of a new millennium. Now is the time to allow God to make us pliable new wineskins, so that we may be involved in a historic move of God to fulfill the Great Commission. As youth workers, we are a key component in reaching a world made up of a majority of young people who are the most likely candidates to make the most important decision of life – how will I respond to Jesus Christ?

May God use us, working together strategically, to make this message of hope as clear and accessible as possible.

Now to him who is able to do immeasurably more than all we ask or imagine, according to his power that is at work within us, to him be glory in the church and in Christ Jesus throughout all generations, forever and ever! Amen.

Ephesians 3:20, 21

Doctrinal Statement

We believe

...the Bible to be the inspired, the only infallible, authoritative Word of God.

...that there is one God, eternally existent in three persons: Father, Son and Holy Spirit.

...in the deity of our Lord Jesus Christ, in His virgin birth, in His sinless life, in His miracles, in His vicarious and atoning death through His shed blood, in His bodily resurrection, in His ascension to the right hand of the Father, and in His personal return in power and glory.

...that for the salvation of lost and sinful man, regeneration by the Holy Spirit is absolutely essential.

...in the present ministry of the Holy Spirit, by whose indwelling the Christian is enabled to live a godly life.

...in the resurrection of both the saved and lost; they that are saved unto the resurrection of life and they that are lost unto the resurrection of damnation.

...in the spiritual unity of believers in Christ.

Strategic Local Church Partnership
Greater Twin Cities

Dan Buschow

Background

In 1990, the picture of the Church in the Minneapolis/St. Paul area was very different than the reality we have today. Back then, to envision Baptist, Lutherans, Independent Charismatics, Evangelical Free, Assemblies of God, Covenant, and many other denominations working together, you would really have to have been quite a dreamer.

But over the past decade, this dream of local churches working in strategic partnership with one another has become a reality in the Greater Twin Cities area. God is raising up people in our communities with a passion to see the Church united in our vision. What is that vision? Twofold: for the Church to collectively pray for every lost person in our community – and to see the Gospel presented in a relevant way to all unsaved people in our area.

When you observe pastors and parachurch leaders praying together regularly – from different denominational, ethnic, and social backgrounds – you realize that our vision can truly come to pass. As these men and women from different backgrounds work together strategically, there is an anticipation that something big is about to happen – and it is happening.

What I've just described is the model, the reality, of the Greater Twin Cities ALLIES. Youth workers, pastors, parachurch ministries, media, business leaders, and evidently, God – all working in partnership to see the Gospel presented to three million people.

This wonder is not only happening in the Greater Twin Cities, but it is happening in cities all across America. Christians are beginning to work together.

I remember walking into Canton, Ohio's Jackson High School in September of 1978 as a new youth pastor, . My heart was filled with compassion and a burden for the youth in that school. As I walked the halls, I began to think about the fact that the youth in my church youth group didn't just come from this one school – they came from several of the many junior high and high schools that surrounded our local church building. It was during this time that God began to instill in me that my ministry should be campus-centered instead of church-centered. I began to realize that America's greatest mission field is the school campus. But with this realization it became apparent that it would take the many other youth workers in our area working together to make an impact. This was the beginning that would lead me down the path toward where we are today. But it was still years away.

In early 1989 I moved my family to the Minneapolis/St. Paul area, excited about a new ministry opportunity working alongside a former mentor. But 6 months later, the roof came crashing down. Within a 2-week period of time the ministry became defunct because of a moral failure with which my friend and mentor had become involved. I was devastated.

New Beginning

Over the next few weeks I prayed and sought God for His divine direction for our lives. As I did, God began to give me a vision for the ALLIES ministries. On December 4, 1989, I took out a sheet of paper and began to write out the vision. That was the beginning. Then I shared the dream with Rachel, my wife. Her response was, "Go for it" – and we did.

After telling our parents and family, I approached an acquaintance who would prove to be critical to making the vision take form. With the dream I felt God had given us, I called to set up an appointment with Dave Landes of Customgraphix, a print company. I shared the vision with him and told him what I needed – letterhead, envelopes, brochures, business cards. There was only one problem – I had no money. But God moved on Dave's heart.

By January 1, 1990, ALLIES was off and running. Armed with our new print materials, we began to broadcast the vision on a larger scale. Our plan was to reach students by networking youth workers together. This networking would take place primarily around high-school assembly motivational events. During these events, we would challenge the young people in attendance to come hear the "rest of the story" later at an off-campus location. Of course, we used this off-campus meeting to present Jesus. It was during these formative stages that I began to meet with other youth workers in our area.

Events continued to transpire that enlarged the scope of the ALLIES vision. In 1991 we worked with Sports Outreach Minnesota and the Billy Graham Association to do outreach work that would culminate at that season's Super Bowl. It was exciting to be involved as 300 churches and organizations began to work together on this project. At the end of the day, over 1000 students came to faith in Christ through assemblies and rallies held all across the state of Minnesota. This type of networking continued – two years later, we did a similar outreach using the NBA All-Star Game as a backdrop.

It was in between these two events that I began to realize something – while the network could work together around an event, we didn't really have a city strategy. I began to ask myself why – I began to ask God why. What was the problem? These were two of the major issues that we identified.

1. Youth workers move and change pastorships. The people that worked on the Super Bowl Outreach were not the same as those working with us on the NBA outreach.

2. Events require many meetings and organizational headaches. Most youth workers don't go into youth ministry to sit in meetings – they are interested in being with and reaching kids.

Taking Shape

However, toward the end of 1993, I had a significant meeting with a few key youth pastors where we began to work our way past these obstacles. This meeting would prove to be the beginning of more focused, strategic youth ministry in our area. We agreed to work together not just on events, but in five key areas of ministry – prayer, networking, and communication, training and equipping, outreach ventures and resources.

Now our future began to take shape as these key youth leaders started making the vision their own. They began meeting regularly, strategizing on how to reach the Greater Twin Cities young people. Through these meetings they began working together strategically, mobilizing youth workers of all denominations. Simultaneously, we began publishing a newsletter entitled *The Networker.* The purpose of this publication was to spread the vision of city-reaching to youth workers throughout our area. Together, the meetings and the newsletter formed a solid base for our ultimate goal: empowering students to reach their peers with Christ.

As local church networks began to spring up and grow around our area, ALLIES began to organize the city into a cohesive, citywide movement. We developed a group of key leaders called the ALLIES Twin Cities Advisory Team. This was a group of representatives from a broad range of locales and denominations. Another group that grew the movement was called Area Contacts. These people came from communities all across a seven county area.

With everyone working together, the synergy really began to develop – and not just a temporary synergy like what we had seen with events; rather, a strategic vision for reaching the Greater Twin Cities. Every time we would share our vision the movement would grow. And it wasn't just me sharing the vision – it was youth workers in every community sharing it with their churches, their friends, their students. And as the dream really started to filter out into the community, people began to get excited about the possibilities.

Events – Beginnings, Not Endings

As the partnership began to really live, an interesting thing occurred – we continued having program events, but these events began to be the starting point for more networking and outreach instead of their conclusion. For example, our efforts surrounding See You at the Pole have been given the name Pole and Beyond. And it's more than just a name. We use this event as a way for youth workers to begin a strategic partnership in their community if they don't currently have a network. In other areas it serves as a kick-off event that will propel them to strategically work together throughout the year. It is also a great time for the new youth workers in an area to get connected right away with other youth workers in their community.

From the Pole and Beyond event alone some interesting things have happened. Instead of having one, large Pole and Beyond meeting, we chose to have several smaller rallies all across the city. Why? Because this takes more involvement and leadership from area youth workers in order to organize these regional rallies. It also allows more students to be able to share about what God did during their See You at the Pole. Rather than only having enough time for 5 or 10 students to share, the Pole and Beyond provides the opportunity for more than 600 students to give testimony. Then ALLIES has a two-hour wrap up on live local radio so the whole city can experience together the excitement about what God has done.

Results

The results of these ongoing partnerships have been nothing short of miraculous... In the past few years we've seen 7,000 students trained in evangelism. I've seen a fire marshal have to intervene because so many students were gathering at a commitment altar. I've seen 82,000 youth pack our Metrodome, over 1,200 churches work together and over 15,000 students make faith decisions. Best of all, we have a follow-up plan for each and every student who comes to Christ – their local church youth pastor. Would these kind of results have taken place without an interconnected web of local churches working in unity as The Church – everyone together building the Kingdom? You be the judge.

Summary

What is the picture of our city today as the result of these kinds of strategies? Synergy, communication, enrollment, unity – in short, we have a movement. We continue to share the concept of what could happen if we all could truly and completely work together. We believe that by bringing youth workers together, we can do more than what we can accomplish alone. >From our work with the youth pastors of our area, this statement has been developed – "If we can do more together, then why together don't we do more?" Simple, but true – obvious, but compelling. With this mantra we will, by God's grace, reach every student, every family, every person in our city with the Good News of Jesus Christ.

Timeline of Youth Ministry Development

1706	A Christian society at Harvard
1780-1800	Sunday School concept created and integrated
1851	The YMCA comes to the US
1881	Christian Endeavor is founded
1875	U.S. Supreme Court requires high school attendance
(circa) 1900	"Adolescence" legitimized
1906	Boy's Club of America is founded
1907	4-H is founded
1910	Camp Fire Girls and Boy Scouts of America are founded
1912	Girl Scouts of America is founded
1933	Miracle Book Club is founded
1940	Young Life is founded
1943	Youth for Christ is founded
1955	FCA is founded
1960s	Local churches experiment with hiring part-time youth directors
1962-1963	U.S. Supreme Court rules unconsitutional prayer and Bible recitation in school
1970s	Progressive local churches begin hiring full-time youth pastors
1970s	Youth ministry networking begins
1980s	Full-time youth pastor becomes a prominent role in the local church
1984	Equal Access Act signed into law
(circa) 2000	Youth ministry partnerships emerge

References

Introduction

1. Bill Bright from his book *How to Make Your Mark*, as quoted by
   Dave Adams, (The Development of Youth Ministry as a
   Professional Career, Doctoral Thesis - Liberty University, 1993,
   page 19

Chapter 1: The Beginning

1. Dave Adams, The Development of Youth Ministry as a
   Professional Career, Doctoral Thesis - Liberty University, 1993,
   page 19

Chapter 2: The Parachurch Phenomenon

1. Dave Adams, The Development of Youth Ministry as a
   Professional Career, Doctoral Thesis - Liberty University, 1993,
   page 52-53
2. Mark Senter III, *The Coming Revolution in Youth Ministry and Its
   Radical Impact on the Church*, (Victor Books: Wheaton, Illinois, 1992)
   page 65
3. Ibid., page 141
4. *That Thing You Do*, 20th Century Fox, October 1996
5. *Prospering Parachurch* Christian Management Report, Nov/Dec
   1998
6. Wesley Willmer, J. David Schmidt and Martyn Smith, *The
   Prospering Parachurch, Enlarging the Boundaries of God's
   Kingdom*, (Jossey-Bass Publishers: San Francisco, California,
   1998) page 10

Chapter 3: The Local Church Responds

1. Mark Senter III, *The Coming Revolution in Youth Ministry and Its
   Radical Impact on the Church*, (Victor Books: Wheaton, Illinois, 1992)
   page 142
2. Ibid., page 142

Chapter 4: The Birth of Networking

1. John Crosby as quoted by Jamie Roach, *Improving KCYFC's Effort To Assist Other Youth Workers,* Thesis 1996, page 10

Chapter 5: Networking Grows Up

1. Search Institute Survey, February 1996

Chapter 6: Dynamic Forces

1. Joel Arthur Barker, *Paradigms, The Business of Discovering the Future,* (Harper Publishers: New York, New York, 1992) page 208
2. Tom Peters, *The Circle of Innovation,* (Alfred A Knopf, New York, 1997) page 4
3. Elizabeth Large, "What's the matter with kids today?" The Baltimore Sun, March 1, 1999
4. George Barna, *The Second Coming of the Church* (Word Publishing: Nashville, 1998) page 180
5. Gerald Celente, *Trends 2000, How to Prepare and Profit From the Changes Of The 21st Century,* (Warner Books: New York, New York, 1997) page 299
6. Reggie McNeal, *Revolution in Leadership, Training Apostles for Tomorrow's Church,* (Abingdon Press: Nashville, 1998) page 22
7. Gerald Celente, *Trends 2000, How to Prepare and Profit from the Changes Of The 21st Century,* (Warner Books: New York, New York 1997) page 299
8. Warren Bennis and Michael Mische, *The 21st Century Organization, Reinventing Through Reengineering,* (Jossey-Bass Publishers: San Francisco, California, 1995) page 25
9. YouthWorker Journal, Jan/Feb 1999, pg. 1 Volume XV Number 3
10. Elizabeth Large, "What's the matter with kids today?" The Baltimore Sun, March 3, 1999

Chapter 7: Declining Denominational Influence and the Perishing Parachurch

1. Wayne Rice, Chap Clark, and others, *New Directions for Youth Ministry* (Group Publishing, Inc., Loveland, Colorado: 1998) page 123
2. Mike Yaconelli, "Where's Your Passion? (Part 1)" <u>Journal of Christian Camping</u>, (Vol. 22, No 2, Issue 22) March-April 1990, page 6
3. Mark Senter III, *The Coming Revolution in Youth Ministry and Its Radical Impact on the Church,* (Victor Books: Wheaton, Illinois, 1992) page 22
4. Tony Jones, <u>YouthWorker Journal</u>, Jan/Feb 2000, page 32, (Vol. 1, No. 3)
5. Dr. Leith Anderson, *A Church for the 21st Century* (Bethany House Publishers: Minneapolis, 1992) page 187
6. Russell Chandler, *Racing Toward 2001,* (Zondervan Publishing House and Harper, San Francisco: Grand Rapids, Michigan, 1992) page 245
7. Reggie McNeal, *Revolution in Leadership, Training Apostles for Tomorrow's Church,* (Abingdon Press: Nashville, 1998) page 18

Chapter 8: Strategic Partnerships

1. <u>Puget Sound Business Journal.</u> Daily Edition, Wednesday, August 6, 1997
2. Mark Senter III, *The Coming Revolution in Youth Ministry and Its Radical Impact on the Church,* (Victor Books: Wheaton, Illinois, 1992) page 156
3. Joel Arthur Barker, *Paradigms, The Business of Discovering the Future* (Harper Publishers: New York, New York, 1992) page 55
4. John R. Harbison and Peter Pekar Jr., *Smart Alliances, A Practical Guide to Repeatable Success,* (Jossey-Bass Publishers: San Francisco, California, 1998) page 25
5. Ibid., page 23
6. Ibid., page 20 - 22
7. <u>Christian Management Report,</u> Nov/Dec 1998, page 11

Chapter 9: Partnership Engineering

1. Peter Senge, *The Fifth Discipline, The Art and Practice of the Learning Organization,* (Doubleday: New York, New York, 1990) page 214
2. Ibid., page 234
3. Ibid., page 234, 235
4. Ken Blanchard and Terry Waghorn, *Mission Possible – Becoming a World Class Organization While There's Still Time,* (McGraw-Hill: New York, 1997) page 3

Chapter 14: A Challenge to Youth Pastors

1. Elizabeth Large, "What's the matter with kids today?" The Baltimore Sun, March 3, 1999
2. Lyle E. Schaller, *The New Reformation* (Abingdon Press: Nashville, 1995) page 75
3. Ibid., page 26
4. Stephen Macchia, *Becoming a Healthy Church,* (Baker Book House, 1999)
5. George Barna, *Generation Next* (Regal Books: Ventura, California, 1995) page 80
6. Ibid., page 80
7. Harvey F. Carey, Wayne Rice, Chap Clark, and others, *New Directions for Youth Ministry* (Group Publishing, Inc.: Loveland, Colorado:, 1998) page 32
8. Dr. Leith Anderson, *A Church for the 21st Century* (Bethany House Publishers: Minneapolis, 1992) page 188
9. Doug Fields, *Purpose Driven Youth Ministry* (Zondervan Publishing House: Grand Rapids, Michigan, 1998) page 106
10. Leith Anderson, *A Church for the 21st Century* (Bethany House Publishers: Minneapolis, 1992) page 192
11. Ed Silvosa, *That None Should Perish, How to Reach Entire Cities for Christ Through Prayer Evangelism* (Regal Books: Ventura California, 1994) page 81

12. Joe Loconte, "*The Bully and the Pulpit*," Policy Review, November-December, 1998

13. Ibid.

14. Wayne Rice, Chap Clark, and others, *New Directions for Youth Ministry* (Group Publishing, Inc.: Loveland, Colorado , 1998) page 85

15. Ibid., page 122

16. Ibid., page 122

17. Richard R. Dunn and Mark H. Senter III, *Reaching a Generation for Christ* (Moody Press: Chicago, 1997) page 308

18. Ibid., page 330

19. Ed Silvosa, *That None Should Perish, How to Reach Entire Cities for Christ Through Prayer Evangelism* (Regal Books, Ventura California, 1994) page 88

Chapter 15: The Next Step: Church Assisting Organizations

1. Ken Blanchard and Terry Waghorn, *Mission Possible - Becoming a World Class Organization While There's Still Time*, (McGraw-Hill: New York, 1997) page 19

2. Peter Senge, *The Fifth Discipline, The Art and Practice of the Learning Organization*, (Doubleday: New York, New York, 1990) page 17

3. Mark Senter III, *The Coming Revolution in Youth Ministry and Its Radical Impact on the Church*, (Victor Books: New York, New York, 1992) page 29

4. Joel Arthur Barker, *Paradigms, The Business of Discovering the Future* (Harper Publishers) page 125

5. Christian Management Report, Nov/Dec 1998, page 11

6. FaithWorks Website, www.faithworks.net , May 27, 1999

7. Warren Bennis and Michael Mische, *The 21st Century Organization, Reinventing Through Reengineering*, (Jossey-Bass Publishers: San Francisco, California, 1995) page 5

8. Ibid., page 4

9. John R. Harbison and Peter Pekar Jr., *Smart Alliances, A Practical Guide to Repeatable Success*, (Jossey-Bass Publishers: San Francisco, California, 1998) page 92

10. Ibid., page 91

11. Tom Peters, *The Circle of Innovation*, (Alfred A Knopf, New York, 1997) page 261

12. Dr. Al Metsker, Founder, Kansas City Youth for Christ

13. <u>Christian Management Report</u>, Nov/Dec 1998, page 11

14. Ibid.

Chapter 16: Overcoming Obstacles

1. Peter Drucker, *Management Challenges for the 21st Century*, (HarperCollins: New York, New York, 1999) page 73

2. Warren Bennis and Michael Mische, *The 21st Century Organization, Reinventing Through Reengineering*, (Jossey-Bass Publishers: San Francisco, California, 1995) page 10

3. Ken Blanchard and Terry Waghorn, *Mission Possible – Becoming a World Class Organization While There's Still Time*, (McGraw-Hill, New York, 1997) Forward

4. Ibid., page 20-21

5. Tom Peters, *The Circle of Innovation*, (Alfred A Knopf, New York, 1997) page 76

6 Ken Blanchard and Terry Waghorn, *Mission Possible - Becoming a World Class Organization While There's Still Time*, (McGraw-Hill: New York, 1997) page 25

7. George Barna, *The Second Coming of the Church* (Nashville: Word Publishing, 1998) page 36

8. Ibid., page 203

9. Quindon Tarver/Lee Perry/ Baz Luhrman, *Everybody's Free to Wear Sunscreen* (Mushroom Records, 1997)

10. Joel Arthur Barker, *Paradigms, The Business of Discovering the Future* (Harper Publishers: New York, New York, 1992) page 69

11. Ken Blanchard and Terry Waghorn, *Mission Possible – Becoming a World Class Organization While There's Still Time*, (McGraw-Hill: New York, New York, 1997) page 175

12. Dr. Leith Anderson, *A Church for the 21st Century* (Bethany House Publishers: Minneapolis, 1992) page 186

13. Peter Senge, *The Fifth Discipline, The Art and Practice of the Learning Organization*, (Doubleday: New York, New York, 1990) page 181

14. Ken Blanchard and Terry Waghorn, *Mission Possible – Becoming a World Class Organization While There's Still Time*, (McGraw-Hill: New York, New York, 1997) page 182

15. Ibid., page 49, 50

16. Ibid., page 50

17. Tom Peters, *The Circle of Innovation*, (Alfred A Knopf: New York, 1997) page 68

18. Gerald Celente, *Trends 2000, How to Prepare and Profit From the Changes of the 21st Century*, (Warner Books: New York, New York, 1997) page 306

19. Ken Blanchard and Terry Waghorn, *Mission Possible – Becoming a World Class Organization While There's Still Time*, (McGraw-Hill: New York, New York, 1997) page 49, 50

20. Reggie McNeal, *Revolution in Leadership, Training Apostles for Tomorrow's Church*, (Abingdon Press: Nashville, 1998) page 33

21. Dr. Leith Anderson, *A Church for the 21st Century* (Bethany House Publishers: Minneapolis, 1992) page 198

22. Wesley Willmer, J. David Schmidt and Martyn Smith, *The Prospering Parachurch, Enlarging the Boundaries of God's Kingdom*, (Jossey-Bass Publishers: San Francisco, California, 1998) page 161

23. Ibid., page 193

24. Dr. Leith Anderson, *A Church for the 21st Century* (Bethany House Publishers: Minneapolis, 1992) page 186

25. George Barna, *The Second Coming of the Church* (Word Publishing: Nashville, 1998) page 130

26. Ibid., page 183

Chapter 17: What Could Happen?

1. Marcel Proust as quoted in *Paradigms, The Business of Discovering the Future*, by Joel Arthur Barker (Harper Publishers: New York, New York, 1992) page 209

2. George Barna, *The Second Coming of the Church* (Word Publishing: Nashville, 1998) page 130

3. Ed Silvosa, *That None Should Perish, How to Reach Entire Cities for Christ Through Prayer Evangelism* (Regal Books: Ventura California, 1994) page 21

4. Dave Adams, The Development of Youth Ministry as A Professional Career, Doctoral Thesis, 1993, page 70

5. Ed Silvosa, *That None Should Perish, How to Reach Entire Cities for Christ Through Prayer Evangelism* (Regal Books: Ventura California, 1994) page 60

6. Ibid., page 142, 143

7. George Barna, *The Second Coming of the Church* (Word Publishing: Nashville , 1998) page 203

8. Ibid., page 53

9. Mark Senter III, *The Coming Revolution in Youth Ministry and Its Radical Impact on the Church*, (Victor Books: Wheaton, Illinois, 1992) page 175

10. Margaret Wheatley, "When Complex Systems Fail: New Roles for Leaders." Leader to Leader, Number 11, Winter 1999, page 34

11. Peter Senge, *The Fifth Discipline, The Art and Practice of the Learning Organization*, (Doubleday: New York, New York, 1990) page 205, 206

12. Wesley Willmer, J. David Schmidt and Martyn Smith, *The Prospering Parachurch, Enlarging the Boundaries of God's Kingdom*, (Jossey-Bass Publishers: San Francisco, California, 1998) page 122

13. George Barna, *The Second Coming of the Church* (Word Publishing: Nashville, 1998) page 63

14. Warren Bennis and Michael Mische, *The 21st Century Organization, Reinventing Through Reengineering*, (Jossey-Bass Publishers: San Francisco, California, 1995) page 45

15. Ed *Silvosa, That None Should Perish, How to Reach Entire Cities for Christ Through Prayer Evangelism* (Regal Books: Ventura California, 1994) Forward
16. Grolier Interactive Encyclopedia Inc, 1998
17. Tom Peters, *The Circle of Innovation*, (Alfred A Knopf: New York, 1997) page 91

Sources

Dr. Leith Anderson, *A Church for the 21st Century* (Bethany House Publishers: Minneapolis, 1992)

Richard R. Dunn and Mark H. Senter III, *Reaching a Generation for Christ* (Moody Press: Chicago, 1997)

Russell Chandler, *Racing Toward 2001*, (Grand Rapids, Michigan: Zondervan Publishing House and Harper: San Francisco, 1992)

Wayne Rice, Chap Clark, and others, *New Directions for Youth Ministry* (Group Publishing, Inc.: Loveland, Colorado, 1998)

Lyle E. Schaller, *The New Reformation* (Abingdon Press: Nashville, 1995)

George Barna, *The Second Coming of the Church* (Word Publishing: Nashville, 1998)

George Barna, *Generation Next* (Regal Books: Ventura, California, 1995)

Wesley Willmer, J. David Schmidt and Martyn Smith, *The Prospering Parachurch, Enlarging the Boundaries of God's Kingdom*, (Jossey-Bass Publishers: San Francisco, California, 1998)

John R. Harbison and Peter Pekar Jr., *Smart Alliances, A Practical Guide to Repeatable Success*, (Jossey-Bass Publishers: San Francisco, California, 1998)

Warren Bennis and Michael Mische, *The 21st Century Organization, Reinventing Through Reengineering,* (Jossey-Bass Publishers: San Francisco, California, 1995)

Ken Blanchard and Terry Waghorn, *Mission Possible – Becoming a World Class Organization While There's Still Time,* (McGraw-Hill, New York, New York, 1997)

Tom Peters, *The Circle of Innovation,* (Alfred A Knope: New York, 1997)

Peter Senge, *The Fifth Discipline, The Art and Practice of the Learning Organization,* (Doubleday: New York, New York, 1990)

Mark Senter III, *The Coming Revolution in Youth Ministry and Its Radical Impact on the Church,* (Victor Books: Wheaton, Illinois, 1992)

Gerald Celente, *Trends 2000, How To Prepare and Profit From the Changes Of the 21st Century,* (Warner Books: New York, New York, 1997)

Joel Arthur Barker, *Paradigms, The Business of Discovering the Future,* (Harper Publishers: New York, New York, 1992)

Ed Silvosa, *That None Should Perish, How to Reach Entire Cities for Christ Through Prayer Evangelism* (Regal Books: Ventura California, 1994)

Reggie McNeal, *Revolution In Leadership, Training Apostles For Tomorrow's Church,* (Abingdon Press: Nashville, 1998)

Recommended Reading – Especially for Youth Pastors

I want to encourage you to read Doug Fields' book,
Purpose-Driven Youth Ministry (Zondervan Publishing House).
Doug does a great job of compiling and communicating information on
the importance of strategic, purpose-driven youth ministry
structure, philosophy and programs.